GET A GRIP

GET A GRIP

Parenting Tips I Wish I'd Known Then

That You Can Know Now

Robin G. Banks

Paige and Steven,
what a wonderful time to have
a family — a gift from God
for sure. I hope you enjoy
GAG and that it helps
make life easier for you.

Robo Press
2214 Hearthstone Drive
Gastonia, N. C. 28056

Merry Christmas and a
safe 2013!

Get A Grip

Cover Illustration by Matt Dorton; Cover Design by Thomas Marketing, Inc.

ISBN: 978-0615662282

Printed and bound in the United States of America.

Robo Press
2214 Hearthstone Drive
Gastonia, N. C. 28056
(704) 867-2126

For more information: robin2214@yahoo.com
www.robingunterbanks.com

To those of you

who remained steadfast over the many years

in your interest in me and my writing. Thank you for caring.

And especially to

my biggest cheerleader—you know who you are—whose

ever-present support and encouraging words I counted on from the

beginning and at every turn. A bucket load of hugs.

Just as my parents did, I left the hospital
as ignorant as our newborn babe.

—Robin Banks

CONTENTS

FOREWORD

Last Valentine's Day, my lovely and most tolerant wife of 43 years (a testament to her tolerance if ever there was one) gave me a card that read "Remember when we first fell in love?" underneath which was "We were so stupid!" It continued inside with "Thanks for growing better with me."

As I read Robin Banks's manuscript, I thought of that card. Willie was 19 when we married. I was 20. We had our first child a year later. She was a teenage mom, just shy of her 20th birthday. We have grown better together, for sure, but oh the problems we could have avoided, or at least handled so much better, if someone with Robin's wisdom had been at our sides, guiding us through the almost inevitable problems involved in trying to peacefully co-exist with another strong-willed human being of the opposite gender.

Like Bill and Robin, Willie and I had different ideas concerning how to raise kids. Keep in mind that America did not yet recognize me as a parenting expert, and let me guarantee you, America recognized me as such long before Willie did. We battled over how to discipline, when to discipline, over what to discipline, and generally over what the meaning of the word *discipline* was in the first place. She was right most of the time, I now realize. Finally, we simply agreed that in parenting matters, I had the right to express my opinion, but she had the final word. By then, though, the kids were teenagers. They were fine, but we all remember battles royal over how to handle them.

Willie and I came from very different backgrounds. Both dysfunctional, mind you, but very different. Her parents stayed together. Mine didn't. My mother remarried when I was seven, to a man who was most definitely not a recommendable human being. Willie's dad was a control freak who couldn't control his own business affairs, much less his kids. And on and on the soap opera goes. To our marriage, we brought vastly different "baggage," as Robin calls it, baggage that constantly got in the way. Sometimes I think Willie and I have only really been married for a decade or so. We've always loved one another with a Romeo and Juliet passion, but it took the better part of 43 years to get it together.

If, early on, we had kindled a relationship with someone older and wiser, like the older and wiser person Robin Banks is today, we could have started being really and truly married about two decades earlier, at least.

Anyway, Robin knows how to heal the junky stuff that goes with marriage and parenting. I'm a psychologist, but she's a commonsensist. I just made that word up. It describes her perfectly. I wish I had her—my mother would have used the term—"horse sense."

Finally, Robin's a regular mom who offers a close-up of her growing pains to spare future and new parents much of the stress and frustration she experienced. Her honesty is sure to help them get a grip on parenthood.

—John Rosemond, Author of *Parenting by The Book*, among others.

\

Comfort Suites (TN527)

BY CHOICE HOTELS

161 W Dumplin Valley, Road
Kodak, TN 37764
(865) 933-3131
GM.TN527@choicehotels.com

PATTERSON, CHARLES
411 EAGLES WALK
GASTONIA, NC 28056

Account:	2612245166
Date:	12/27/12
Room:	420 ssc
Arrival Date:	12/26/12
Departure Date:	12/27/12
Check In Time:	12/26/12 8:30 PM
Check Out Time:	
Rewards Program ID:	
You were checked out by:	
You were checked in by:	pbritt.tn527
Total Balance Due:	**0.00**

Post Date	Description	Comment	Amount
12/26/12	Room Charge	#420 PATTERSON, CHARLES	67.05
12/26/12	State Tax		6.54
12/26/12	Occupancy Tax		2.01
12/27/12	Visa Payment	XXXXXXXXXXXXX0559	(75.60)

Folio Summary 12/26/12 - 12/26/12

	Amount
Room Charge	67.05
State Tax	6.54
Occupancy Tax	2.01
Visa Payment	(75.60)

Balance Due: **0.00**

INTRODUCTION

It Began in a Garden

Because of the apple debacle, Adam and Eve destined mankind to bear and rear children outside Eden's gates. Consequently, they forfeited what could have been a perfect life of familial bliss. Instead, they faced an unfamiliar reality of pain and chaos, which prompted me to ask the question: Were they good parents?

I couldn't say. As the alpha couple, they had no earthly resources on which to rely: no parents or friends, no psychologists or certified counselors, no seminars or retreats, no books or the Internet. In a very real sense, they had an excuse not to prepare. Today's future parents do not.

Although I'm in my sixties and on the far side of parenting, I see preparation as an obvious course, particularly after posing questions like these: Would I jump into a pond without swimming lessons? Would I attempt to create tiramisu without a recipe? Would I try out for Phantom of the Opera without acting lessons? No, no, and absolutely no. So why not prepare for the most challenging yet worthwhile job in existence?

Get a Grip: Parenting Tips I Wish I'd Known Then That You Can Know Now doesn't proclaim news breaking information—failsafe techniques, miraculous solutions—however, if uninformed, you will definitely find what you read beneficial. The book supplies a basic knowledge that will point you in the direction of effective parenting.

How anyone can argue against preparation is beyond me. When the rabbit died, yesterday's lingo for today's plus sign on a home pregnancy test, I gobbled up everything—books, magazine articles, tidbits from friends—on the bodily changes I would experience and on what to expect when the big day came.

I would lose my waistline within weeks, throw up my Frosted Flakes for the first trimester, and at term be unable to climb stairs without panting. I read in paralyzing detail about needles and nerve-blocking options as well as the three stages of labor. I learned that the cheese-like substance covering my newborn was not some moldy residue that could harm this perfect child. These things were normal and shouldn't freak me out. Had my arms been long enough, I could have delivered my own baby.

Then suddenly I was holding my daughter. After two days in the hospital, not the week my mother had enjoyed, the nurse rolled us into the sunlight. We were expected to return home and become a perfectly bonded mother and child. Whoa, ho-ho. The baby in my arms was crying, and I had no idea what to do.

Preparing for parenthood was unheard of in my parents' generation and in the ones before theirs. Like everyone else, I thought I would be different. And like everyone else, I had been so caught up in the wonderment of pregnancy that I never thought about what came next. Just as my parents had, I left the hospital as ignorant as my newborn babe, though not as innocent. I really could and should have been better prepared.

Time slipped in and out of crowded days, months, and years without my realizing it. One minute my firstborn was in diapers and the next she was headed to college leaving two teenage brothers in her wake.

I had lived half a century. My life swerved in a new direction, and I don't mean menopause because that monster had been chewing on me for nearly a decade. A parent-child showdown with my teenage sons ignited a spark I had nurtured since childhood: write a book.

The life-altering challenge my boys dumped on my unsuspecting person meant I would no longer be their self-appointed academic dean. Can you imagine?! I would have to relinquish that position—a role guaranteed to all moms in the universal motherhood pledge— and with it a huge amount of control over their lives. I succumbed to their demands, a timely flash of insight no doubt. And with the same certainty that I had done the right thing, I knew I had to take action: I would record key lessons and truths of motherhood for my children and other prospective parents.

My background includes a B.A. in secondary education and an M.A. in Spanish. I hold no diplomas in psychology, counseling, or childcare to adorn the walls of my newly outfitted office. Since the space had formerly been my son's bedroom, miles of wire had been taped to the walls and ceiling to provide a pleasant surround-sound system. Although not my idea of chic decorating, I somehow knew that tolerance of my son's resourcefulness, regardless of how it manifested itself, would preserve any other creative spark that might be lurking around his teenage brain.

My restraint in the face of flawed interior design stands as proof of my true credentials: on the job experience with a desire to help through an honest assessment of that experience. During the writing of this book, I developed a stark understanding of the importance of trusting your common sense rather than justifying your actions with lame excuses and ignoring your God-given firewall of good sense. Armed with the wish that I'd known then what you can know now, I put my ideas on paper.

This book and its future sequel *Get a Grip II* became my passion. I wanted Dede, Andy, and Mark to have the benefit of my hindsight so they could more efficiently navigate the waters I had slogged through up to the waist. Having a look around the corner before they turned the corner and walked down the block would give them more self-confidence. And it might ease their fears of the unknown.

I want you future and new parents, too, to know what I didn't know when I began raising my family of one husband, three children, two dogs, multiple stray cats, assorted tropical fish, one pink Easter chick, a token rodent-type varmint, and in-season hermit crabs. My favorite proverb "An ounce of prevention is worth a pound of cure" rings in my ears like church bells on Christmas morning.

My warrior cry is: Get a grip! Reading about my life under fire will guarantee that grip on parenthood by giving you a much needed head start toward the goal of sound parenting. I'm convinced that giving serious thought to how to parent, especially before that twinkle in a spouse's eye becomes a larger-than-life reality, swaddled in a receiving blanket topped with a pink or blue watch cap, will make life easier, less stressful. I say less stressful rather than stress-free because anyone who has had a teenager has had to suffer his "I-am-me-and-gotta-be-free" attitude.

Examining my past was like looking through night-vision goggles at nocturnal forest life. It opened my eyes and sharpened my vision, enabling me to see and understand subtle stirrings and behaviors I didn't see and understand when I was on the job. Now you can use my clarity to break up the fog of your uncertainty.

This book will show you, for example, how coming to terms with your spouse on parenting strategies benefits both you and your child.

You'll also witness the resulting confusion and chaos when couples parent separately. Your eyes will be opened to the presence of emotional baggage you transported from your childhood into your marriage and how this baggage, if not dealt with, affects parenting techniques.

Parenting is like no other job in this universe; it places an utmost responsibility on your shoulders. You'll see how having all systems on go, how replacing ignorance with knowledge increases your odds of crossing the finish line with fewer wrinkles, the satisfaction of a race well run, and the comfort that you've left our planet in the capable hands of the next generation.

By clarifying my strengths and weaknesses, I am able to help you prepare your children to be productive members of society and to live healthy lives. My weathered wisdom was acquired from two and a half decades of parental growing pains. Every parent experiences these growing pains which can be better handled if you dine on a steady diet of nutritious preparation.

Before I began writing this book, I found shelves and shelves of material at the bookstores. Some of the books were so technical it was paralyzing. Only eleven specially educated Americans and God could have understood them.

The concerns that had mattered most to me as a parent had to be pared down and conveyed in simple language. My analysis of my experiences would be heartfelt and anecdotal. Stories teach best. I want to be heard as an ordinary mom by all moms, dads too, who want the best for their children.

I chose six areas of concern for this first book: establishing a united front, claiming emotional baggage, setting a good example, crafting good rules, requiring accountability, and creating family traditions. I then put the Banks family on the big screen to show how effective (or not) my husband and I had been as our children's caretakers. This book is a close-up of our successes and mistakes in HD without air brushing. It also suggests where to begin, what to expect, and how to cope before you find yourself too far out on that well-worn limb.

Perfect or even close-to-perfect parents don't exist. I know that now. So although my hindsight is 20/20, it shouldn't be taken as the absolute cure for less-than-sound parenting. Raising children is not an exact science. I assure you that in the deluge of information on parenting no official blueprint has yet surfaced. Every family is unique. Parenting can't be reduced to a standard recipe; more than one way exists to prepare tasty Italian spaghetti.

At best, parenting is like the Cyclone roller coaster ride. It's exhilarating, but unexpected dips, eighty-five-degree drops, and sharp curves are part of its nature. Before you get on the ride, prepare as much as possible and decide to handle the journey with a love that nurtures, that is patient and kind, as well as a love that disciplines and teaches. You have eighteen years—a click of the mouse when compared to a lifetime—to gift your children the roadmap for abundant living.

Finally, take comfort in knowing that you are not alone. Take advantage of seminars and classes, counselors and clergy, the Internet and books, anything and anyone who can broaden your perspective. Better yet, keep God in the picture. Prayer is as close as your next breath. A child is a gift from Him; therefore, it is a privilege to be a parent. To be an effective parent is in turn a gift to your child.

Break the cycle of all the generations before you. Prepare. Imagine the ripple-effect of healthier parenting *you* can create for future generations.

CHAPTER ONE

UNITED WE STAND
Parenting as a Team

The gray Topaz pulled into the carport right before six o'clock. Our golden retriever, Liquor, had been lounging on the cool cement faithfully waiting for his master to arrive home. He sprang to his feet, tail wagging like a high-speed metronome, until my husband got out of the car.

After squatting down to scratch the family pet, Bill braced for the onslaught of our three young children. The screen door flew open with cries of "Daddy! Daddy!" and "Me first!" After hugging and kissing each child, Bill opened the door, dropped his paperwork on the washer, and found me in the kitchen. I stopped cleaning the sink long enough to get my perfunctory hug and kiss. With three children swarming about, any hope that he might ravish my bod was out of the question.

As he peeked through the oven door, I cornered him, "How was your day? Did you get the big order you were talking about last night?"

Thinking that was an adequate greeting, I then unloaded all my woes. I was minutes away from getting supper on the table and knew I had to grab my personal gardener before he went outside to survey the yard for any weeds that might have popped up overnight.

"Andy wouldn't listen," I said. "Dede picked at him the entire afternoon." Because I wasn't sure hubby was focused on what I was saying, I lead him into the living room. "Look, Mark finger-painted with ketchup all over the carpet. Say something to them."

Bill poured himself a glass of iced tea, and then leaned against the counter. "I don't see why you can't handle the kids by yourself."

* * *

What had Bill and I been thinking when we'd had our first child, a baby girl we'd named Dede, after my mother? Clearly we hadn't given one iota of thought to how we would run our household. Because everything had gone so smoothly in the beginning, I never dreamed we wouldn't parent as a team, much less that this opening scene would be replayed over and over.

Each time it did, I was frustrated with Bill's response yet too exhausted to thoughtfully continue the discussion. Without changing the dialogue, how could I expect to find a different reply or reach some middle ground? Instead, I would talk myself into giving solo parenting one more try. After all, my mother had looked after three young children by herself while my father had traveled during the week. *If she could do it, so could I,* the challenge I would fall back on every time Bill and I repeated the weary conversation of that opening scene. It was true my life would be easier if I could settle minor disputes and discipline the children by myself, particularly when Bill was physically absent.

Getting to Know Your Spouse

After Dede's birth, Bill and I were up to our armpits in diapers and you-know-what before I noticed our different ways of doing things. Bill, an Army veteran, was an efficiency expert. With swift, economic movements he could strip off a diaper, swab and powder the behind, secure a new diaper, fold and tape the soiled one into a compact roll, and then toss it into the garbage can in under a minute. Dede was trussed up like a cotton bale without possibility of fall-out. I, however, viewed the task more as a playtime than a job to be completed. I talked and sang to her until she was secure in a fresh diaper.

Another routine Bill and I approached differently was our young sons' nightly bath. If I was finishing up in the kitchen, Bill would bathe the guys. If he was helping Dede with homework, I would bathe them. It was all quite civilized, and neither of us realized we were operating as a team.

Knowing that cleanliness was next to godliness, I gave each child his own washcloth. With Andy, I used the Spiderman washrag; with Mark, I used his duck mitten. I assumed Bill did likewise until the evening I saw him move swiftly from one kid to the next using the same cloth.

"It's quicker and easier," he said.

No big deal. The boys were getting clean and that was priority number one.

It turned out that it had indeed been a big deal for four-year-old Mark. Years later at a Christmas dinner Mark regaled us with a story about bath time with Dad: Andy, six or seven at the time, stood in the tub while Mark played with a toy motorboat.

"Dad, why is Andy always first?" Mark said.

"I don't know. I guess it's a habit . . . he's the oldest." Bill soaped up the rag and began to scrub Andy from top to bottom until his body glistened pink.

"Your turn." Bill leaned over the tub toward Mark.

"Get my mitten," the younger brother instructed.

"I'll turn the rag over."

"But that's been all over Andy's—"

"Son, I turned it over. See? Now stand up."

Mark had everyone in tears as he narrated how Dad began washing his face, going from stem to stern just like he had done with Andy. He demonstrated how tightly he'd squeezed his eyes and mouth shut as Spiderman slid over his face. Mark swore that the Papster, the children's affectionate name for their dad, could never wash away the image of his face being cleaned with the same cloth that seconds before had toured Andy's danger zone.

* * *

Because our early operating differences evolved more around the children's physical needs than emotional concerns, such as obedience, character, and spiritual growth, they created no real problems. We loved each other and were more amused by our differences than forewarned by them. It never entered our brains that they might signal differing parenting styles and attitudes.

Had we done a minimum of prep-work before children by asking key questions to determine where we stood on certain child-rearing issues, we would have discovered them in time to deal with them calmly. Instead, we were later surprised by them. When that terrible day came, sanity and goodwill toward men took a downward turn.

Bill and I were products of our parents. Like his father, he was not keen on working as a parental team. Not being a planner by nature, he took care of things as they happened. On the other hand, I, like my mother, favored organization. I enjoyed making plans and dealing with potential problems ahead of time.

Not only had we been influenced by our parents, we were also subject to our genetic wiring. During the family years, Bill generally behaved like the mild-mannered Mr. Rogers, a beloved children's TV personality. When a disagreement arose with the children, he approached it logically and calmly. He listened and asked questions that went to the core of the problem. Patience and respect were far more persuasive than angry demands. I, on the other hand, marched in like Attila the Hun with club raised, ready to do battle.

It was just a matter of time before our mindsets and temperaments collided, leaving conflict and frustration littering the battlefield.

Elementary Years

When there was only one child, an easily disciplined daughter, I succeeded in maintaining order. With the addition of a second and third, particularly two rambunctious boys, Bill's theory that I alone should be able to run a tight ship quickly sprung a leak. Before long the kids knew I was the lone captain without any reinforcement. If they held out long enough, they would be able to sink the ship. We all know what happens to the captain when the ship goes down.

Being an at-home mother juggling kids from preschool to elementary ages, I frequently found myself two steps away from total meltdown. All efforts at consistency and reason were buried under a minefield of toys, Picasso-inspired food creations, and lakes of spilled beverages.

My last thread of sanity disintegrated when ceaseless whining and the constant pick, pick, picking of the children at one another escalated into total chaos. Calgon's "Take me away" bath commercial was still a fantasy in some advertiser's mind. Who had time anyway? Teetering between deserting and volunteering for kamikaze duty, I found myself frantically searching the backyard for the burly men who would whisk me away to the psycho ward.

Desperation oozed from every pore of my body. I mentioned to Bill that our church was offering parenting classes. But, while I would bare my soul to a Salvation Army bell ringer, Bill's reticence in opening up, though more dignified than having a counseling session with a charity worker, didn't help us get a grip on the issues. He preferred not to air our personal problems via group discussions. When I failed to convince him that we needed help, I went anyway.

Hysteria bubbled below the surface when I discussed my dilemma. It was comical. Obviously everyone knew that "my husband" was Bill, so much for being discreet. The psychologist confirmed my belief that husband and wife should be a united front. The kids had to learn and believe we were.

If we were to parent together, he also said we must stand together in our decisions, the execution of house rules, and with verbal support for each other. From the time we had started our family, I had desperately needed the kids to know with the same certainty that they would attend church on Sunday morning that their dad, who commanded instant obedience with one stern look or the "I'm-only-saying-this-once" tone of voice, backed me one hundred percent. I wanted them to imagine, especially during his absence, a life-size cardboard cut-out of him next to me. The head would be on a spring and would bob up and down at my every word.

I needed Bill's input; I wanted us to find solutions based on both our ideas. Regardless of what I said or what I told him the psychologist had said, I couldn't persuade him to parent as one. He didn't get it. He didn't budge.

Although I didn't know it at the time, Bill was merely reenacting the way his father had managed his own household. The past had him in a viselike grip. Between the lack of a united front and having to care for three children and a husband, I often felt like a rocket ship in turbulent weather without a copilot or a destination.

Favorite Diversionary Tactic of the Young and the Crafty

Still not reaching an understanding with Bill regarding our different behavioral traits and parenting ideas, I trudged ahead anyway. What else could I do? I hoped it would all work out, obviously blind to the potholes in our future. We hit one of those potholes hard when Mark, then around five or six years old, worked his magic one Saturday morning. I was in the utility room switching clothes from the washer to the dryer while he sat on the couch in the den.

"Mark," I said, "you need to bring your dirty clothes to the laundry room."

"I'll do it in a minute." His eyes were nailed to the cartoons on TV.

"Mark, I need all the dirty clothes right now."

"How 'bout one more second?'

I left the laundry room and stood between him and the TV. "I said no and I mean no."

"Aw, Mom, I'm right in the middle of my program. Just five more minutes. I promise I'll get my stuff. I promise."

"You heard me. Right now!"

I shot him the pursed-lips, narrowed-eyes look as I toted a basket of clean clothes to the other side of the house. The minute I disappeared, Bill passed through the den. He was dressed in yard clothes and headed to the kitchen to look for a tool he'd misplaced. Mark zapped him.

"Hey, Dad, Mom says I have to get my dirty clothes right now and my program's not over, so can I please wait 'til then? Pleeze, Dad. It's just a few more minutes."

Bill located the screwdriver, and making a beeline for the back door, gave his son the thumbs up saying: "Yeah, OK. Don't forget."

Thirty minutes later Mark was still watching TV.

* * *

The formula for this scene is simple: child gets a no from one parent and then asks the other for a reprieve. The child, in effect, bobs and weaves. When that happened, I often felt like the cartoon character Wile E. Coyote who spends much of his life flattened out on the highway due to some Road Runner scheme. In my case, I was leveled by parenting ignorance.

Mark zeroed in on our natural state of bustling activity, planning the next move that would get him whatever he desired. You may say I've gone too far in thinking that a five- or six-year-old could be so calculating. I have not. I now realize these precious babes are hard-wired in the womb to bob-and-weave from the moment they make their grand appearance into the delivery room. Mark put the bob-and-weave technique into practice that Saturday morning, thus proving this tactic remains key for all kids, because it gets them exactly what they want.

The breakdown occurred in two areas. First, Bill and I were too busy to make sure the task was accomplished. Second, though not entirely related but just as important, Bill could have won points with me by telling Mark, "Obey your mom," golden words that would have felt like landing on a pile of plush fur. Alas, teamwork was handicapped by our unwillingness to sacrifice our time to pause long enough to follow through.

Parents who don't address the issue at hand and who don't stick together are subject to having their kids play them against each other. Those who do communicate can avoid the games and end the discussion early. Offspring might think twice before objecting to a parental decision when Mama's instruction and Dad's represent one firm voice.

If the situation escalates to an argument with the child, spousal backup can diffuse an otherwise impossible conflict. It also confirms that you're not alone on the job, and that in turn lessens spousal discord. This understanding by both parents and children tilts the playing field in favor of the big people. It also energizes the marital relationship.

Knowing about the bob-and-weave technique offers a certain degree of protection from being blindsided by your little darlings. However, it's unwise to get cocky just because you're aware of the technique. If teamwork isn't in place, you can still crumble to their machinations. I recommend staying on high alert, presenting a united front, and sticking to your little kids like metal to a magnet until you get the desired results.

Another Pothole

A common foible, and one that Bill and I failed to recognize, is procrastination. This parenting pothole further jeopardizes hope for a united front. Sometimes a token exchange was all Bill and I could muster when our children disobeyed the TV rule about program selection. I remember the evening when I reported to him Mark's failure to comply:

"Mark was watching Sally Jessy Raphael this afternoon," I said when I heard Bill come through the garage door. "I sent him to his room."

"Ya mean that talk-show woman with the red glasses?" My husband went straight to the fridge.

"Bill, did you hear me? Dishtowel in hand, I turned around from the sink to face him. I knew he'd had a long day at work and his mind was elsewhere, but I needed his help. "I said Mark was watching Sally Jessy. Will you talk to him?"

"Hey, can we do this after supper? I need to mow the grass before we leave for the game this weekend."

"Don't forget," I said, knowing full well there was a good chance we'd do just that.

* * *

Mark, way too impressionable at the tender age of nine or ten, was mesmerized by talk shows, especially those that covered everything from transvestites to orgies. He wasn't old enough to be exposed to that side of life . . . I'm not sure I was.

Bill and I never got around to having a conversation, so we tabled it, which is where it remains today. Helping with homework, cleaning the kitchen, tending the yard, and simply forgetting, because discussing similar issues wasn't top priority, often allowed similar scenarios to pass without resolution.

This is not acceptable. Being consistent in discussing the issues at hand will require extreme effort, but I promise you it pays off down the road. Pushing through your exhaustion or writing yourself a reminder note or simply stopping what you're doing comes with being a good parent. You can slack up when your children leave home; hopefully, they'll leave home.

Teen Years: Television Troubles

The TV dilemma clearly illustrated the lack of synchronization between Bill and me. A TV rule had been in place since the kids had entered preschool. In the early days I allowed them to watch educational programs like Sesame Street, Mister Rogers, and The Electric Company. I didn't mind if they watched the occasional TV special featuring Charlie Brown or some other seasonal show.

Then they went to big school, the elementary level, and gradually added more programs to their preferred viewing. Sit-coms, talk shows, and sports events were on their must-see lists. But programs like Jerry Springer, The Simpsons and Married with Children were not on mine. The kids were too young, the subjects too distasteful, and the characters too disrespectful.

Dede rarely watched as much TV as the boys. By the time the guys entered teen-hood, they had built an unholy alliance with the home entertainment unit. They spent countless hours if not watching it then playing electronic games with handheld sets surgically connected by thousands of wires to a big black box—passing through the den was hazardous to everyone's health. The boys were so attached to the appliance that I could have plugged the vacuum cleaner into their bellybuttons had there been a power outage.

I became obsessed about the downside of their TV watching: their IQ's would plummet to that of a can of paint. I wanted them to read or do some other activity, but they refused. I grew tired of being the heavy all the time. "You're so mean," they often said, and I at times gave in. I learned to ignore manipulative remarks like that—and that's all they were—much too late.

After one particularly hectic day, I entered the den only to gaze upon two bona fide potato heads, their multiple eyes bulging and fixed on the boob tube. That image brought me to the breaking point.

"Listen up, everybody!" I ordered. "There's a new two-hour-a-day TV rule. That means no TV before supper and no shows with sex, violence, or bad language."

This edict permitted age-appropriate viewing, for example, weather and news reports, Tide commercials, re-runs of Leave It to Beaver, and limited sports programs. I was fixated on my cause.

"And one more thing," I said. "Homework must be finished in the afternoon if you want TV time at night."

Bill reluctantly agreed to my mandate after I told him the boys were becoming couch potato zombies. Honest-to-goodness teamwork was on the horizon. After several days of their unceasing objections without success—Bill was hanging tough with Project TV—the boys adjusted. Dede accepted the change without complaint. To my delight, on several occasions I spied the guys playing board games together after supper. Now that was a sight to behold. They were actually getting along and, dare I say, bonding.

* * *

The kids followed the TV rule for several weeks. I was closely overseeing both the situation and Bill. Everything was going smoothly. I was pleased until I returned home from the grocery store one fateful day. While walking through the den, my maternal radar was picking up unusual vibes.

The boys were nowhere to be seen or heard. I glanced at the television, which stood blankly against the wall. I placed my hand on top. Warmth. Busted.

I cornered Bill and threatened to sell his golf clubs if we didn't discuss the incident. We decided to revoke the boys' TV privileges for a week, from a Tuesday to Tuesday. It was a rare, praiseworthy moment when we practiced teamwork. It felt like that life-is-good bear hug your toddler surprises you with just when you need it most.

Several days passed with the weekend looming ahead, which brought an onslaught of the kids begging me to reinstate regulated, TV worship, at least for the weekend. Any program was better than nothing. While I remained firm in the joint decision Bill and I had made, it soon became apparent that you-know-who had not.

The weekend arrived. On Saturday morning, I left early to run errands. When I returned home later that afternoon, I found the guys watching a basketball game with their father. I was slack-jawed. Bill had just mowed the lawn, edged the driveway, trimmed the hedges, and potted the front porch urns with springtime flowers. The boys, knowing their father was tired and their mother absent, had mentioned to him that sports programs were educational, age-appropriate programs. He wilted.

Seeing the Banks men lined up on the couch with their eyes riveted to the screen, I knew the anger boiling through my veins could have broken the needle on a blood pressure cuff. Instead of asking permission, the boys had bided their time to take advantage of their father's weakened mental state. What he wanted was an ice-cold beer and a place to rest without a lot of chatter. He wanted a good basketball game, not a debate.

On a subconscious level, Bill and I knew the boys were playing us against one another, but we never discussed it. No conversation between us explored his bombing out, either. Be it known here and now that we both failed at TV management and are responsible for our young adults' present-day addiction to it.

This TV obsession became the forerunner to the first hand-held, computer game addiction. These compact forms of entertainment naturally flowed into today's all consuming electronic devices, going beyond the helpful access to one another and the procuring of valuable information to sabotaging one's ability to be patient and to feel secure in being alone. Being disconnected from friends for any length of time is unthinkable in this twenty-first millennium.

Everywhere you go you see how the abuse of and addiction to these gizmos negatively affect our safety, common sense, and good manners as far as when and where to use them. When your child texts while driving or in the classroom or anywhere someone is formally speaking or totes the latest and the coolest device into the john--just in case--wouldn't you say things have gotten out of hand? Parents today are faced with this tremendously challenging lifestyle of the young—and not so young—and restless. This addiction to the flurry of new and constantly improved forms of electronic communication and entertainment is a book in itself. For now, limit TV time and monitor its subject matter; use common sense in the use of today's electronic devices and tomorrow's.

Bob-and-Weave and TV: Thorns in Our Sides

These TV disagreements became commonplace. Bill was out of the picture on TV monitoring. Lacking confidence to stay the course alone, I wavered between enforcing the rule and not. Eventually I not only dropped the ball, I burst it. If Bill had been as passionate about TV viewing as he had been about oral hygiene and grades, surely the unflattering fluorescent glow encircling his sons' heads would have gotten his attention.

Our fragile united front sustained a big hit during the TV campaign. I wasn't looking for perfection, just enough success for the boys to believe we meant business. They needed to learn to respect our decisions, to keep their word, and to become responsible young men. Showing up each morning committed to effective parenting is the hardest work you'll ever undertake. But you sign up for that work when you decide to have a family. "Anything worth doing is worth doing well" should not be taken as mere lip service to a nice idea. Put this philosophy into practice.

Journeying to the past served as a wonderful source of enlightenment. It not only identified the bob-and-weave maneuver, it also clarified that children enter the world with a divide-and-conquer potential; God's sense of humor still baffles many parents today. Our boys' innate ability to bob and weave and divide and conquer, made easier by our shaky united front, became stronger as they grew. Cleverness and slippery tongues labeled them future politicians. Yikes. Like kudzu, their fame grew to legendary status within a three-block radius of our house as they wielded their powers against the neighborhood moms and dads.

Bill and I gave them ample opportunity to hone their craft because we maintained the status quo: separation of powers along with a failure to follow through and communicate. When we didn't come up with a conscious plan of action, our subconscious plan took charge: go straight down the road until you see a curve, hit the curve without braking and hope you make the turn. Frequently, we ran off into the ditch.

As interesting as it may seem, I can't recall Dede's ever plying these manipulating tactics. Children come to us hard-wired with their own temperaments. It appears that certain children are easy to raise while others are more difficult. These differences in their desire to please and use of diversionary tactics in no way excuse parents from getting their act together.

Success with the United Front

The mountain and its seemingly impossible slope toward teamwork cast its lingering shadow on Bill and me. But my need to secure a united front for the welfare of our children was not going away no matter how steep the climb. I would keep the faith. Bill and I could and would team up, at least, to some degree. I had to live this hope. My eternal optimism spurred me on in spite of our less-than-commendable record.

My faith and hope were tested the last week of Andy's eighth-grade year. A certain teacher's key ring disappeared. Andy and a classmate had swiped the keys and made copies. After talking with my son, I learned that he and his buddy hadn't planned to use the keys for a malicious purpose, such as breaking into the band room to wreak havoc or play a prank on a teacher. Possession of the key ring was the end goal. They were in junior high and thought the caper would elevate their status with the ninth graders.

Andy received a three day in-school suspension. As a former high-school Spanish teacher, I knew how important it was to support the staff and for Andy to see me doing so. I called Bill at work to discuss the incident. We agreed that our actions would be a big factor in shaping our son's character. That night we talked with him.

He admitted what he'd done, but there was a problem. The suspension started on Friday, the last day of the school year. The principal wanted to let the punishment slide, but I disagreed. Andy had done something wrong and needed to pay for it. Bill and I agreed that he would comply with the disciplinary measure beginning at 8:00 Monday morning, his first day of summer vacation.

The principal gave Andy his work assignment. For three days he helped the school janitors take out trash, paint, and mop the floors. He worked hard and did so without complaining. He became friends with Toppy and Mike, whose friendship he enjoyed the following year. He handled the growth experience with unexpected maturity. I was proud of my son. And I was proud of Bill and me too. We had pulled together to make a good decision.

Teen Years: Mark

Mark's arrival at high school brought improvement in another area. I had acquired a second layer of skin by then and could stand firm on decisions and consequences. I had also gained some ground with bringing Bill onto the team. Since Andy and Mark were two and a half years apart, I used the distance between them to gain hindsight from Andy's adventures. I thought this gave me a head's-up for a second round with Mark. I donned my breastplate of knowledge, pulled down my face shield of practice, and stood ready to right the wrongs.

It was no time before my prior experience with Andy was put to the test. Mark broke curfew. Bill and I grounded him and impounded his car for a week. We had quickly decided on this consequence in front of him. Being a typical teenager, he had a few things to say:

"But how am I going to get to school?"

"Why don't you give Steve a call?" I said.

"I don't feel comfortable doing that. You know he's always late." Mark's habit was to arrive early to school to avoid any chance of getting a tardy mark. "I just won't go to school," he declared. "I'll be counted as absent."

"That's fine with me." I spoke without wavering. My imaginary pompoms shook in the air. He was playing me.

"Ah, give me a break this one time. It won't happen again. I promise."

"I won't change my mind."

"You're so unfair. Like you never made a mistake!" He spun around, and then thundered his way upstairs.

Mark took pride in his excellent attendance record. More important, too many tardies and absences in high school meant a loss of exam exemptions. With that at stake, I didn't think he would risk missing even one day. Nevertheless, I braced myself against his anger and his promises to do better. If he missed school, so be it. It was up to him to figure out how to get there.

Bill mentioned I could take Mark over to his buddy's house each morning to save time. No. I remained fixed in our decision and believed that my husband would remain strong too. The following day, he drove Mark to his friend's house.

Monster fireworks exploded in my head. Luckily for Bill, my recently created mantra for such crises was up and running: Stay cool. Keep it together. I slipped into the zone of self-restraint. Whatever conversation had passed between father and son, I had been totally undermined. Even more important, our carefully constructed teamwork had crumbled like the walls of Jericho with a blast of our son's trumpet.

* * *

We should have talked privately about Mark's breaking curfew. Then we could have thoroughly discussed the situation without interruption. If I detected any hesitation from Bill, I could have required a blood pact to seal our decision. Nobody in his right mind breaks a promise sealed in blood; ask any former member of a backyard boys' club. Bill's caving on the follow-through reinforced Mark's belief that if he hung in there long enough he would gain a partial concession, if not everything he wanted.

Along the road, life often gets in the way of our good intentions. There were times we relented. In this case, life grabbed Bill by the throat and cut off the air supply to his brain. We could have salvaged something from his desertion had we discussed the collapse of our united front with our son. Call me naïve, but I believe our high school senior would have appreciated his dad's admitting he'd made a mistake.

Nevertheless, all was not lost as I first thought. I had remained calm but firm during the entire ordeal. I was able to do that because Bill and my experience with Andy taught me that everyone would benefit when both parents followed through. That gave me the emotional edge I needed to remain steady—even though Bill hadn't—and to face Mark's heated response and Bill's wavering. Mark figured out how to get to school on his own for the rest of the week.

Afterwards, Bill finally admitted to me he'd missed a chance to teach Mark how to solve his own problems. He also recognized that he'd weakened my authority. From then on we talked more when a problem arose with one of the children. He was beginning to understand the benefit of sharing our opinions and working together . . . and the dark clouds broke open, sunlight came pouring through, the curtain fell. Applause followed.

Devising a game plan as simple as let's talk about it at 7:00 tonight, and following through, regardless of what comes up, reduce stress and frustration. You can then head off out-of-control conflict and chaos, especially when the plan is specific and both parents are committed. All things considered, including my being the eternal optimist, the united front received a booster shot of adrenalin from my being steady and Bill's being enlightened.

Teamwork

You might raise your eyebrows at the difficulties Bill and I faced in achieving teamwork. *These people are educated and smart*, you might think. *What took them so long to figure out how to raise three good kids?*

We knew nothing about practical psychology and family dynamics when we started our family. We knew even less about how we would respond to reality as individuals. We didn't know how to be a successful team. When we began raising our family, I had assumed that we would stand together because I wanted us to.

Don't assume anything. You and your spouse will disagree. Deciding to practice teamwork is just the beginning. To establish credibility and authority, you must talk and not walk. Mutual support after good communication—like biting your tongue and respecting your spouse—is paramount to good decision-making and parenting in general.

Periodic pep talks will ensure you're staying in touch and backing up each other. They will help you stay on track with the important decisions you make. And yielding to your mate's opinion once in a while goes a long way to steering the marriage away from a collision course. Compromise promotes goodwill; it's a skill you want your children to see and adopt.

A united front, although a bit shaky and intermittent, did improve daily life at the Banks home. On those occasions when we worked together and supported one another, it was magic. Frustration burned away like morning fog over a placid lake. Order replaced chaos. Authority without confusion was the rule of the day; I regained credibility and earned respect. I found comfort in having Bill to lean on. Before, all I had wanted to do was lock myself in the bathroom and drown my frustration in a three-day shower.

To be sure, disagreements continued. But generally speaking, the Banks home environment had calmed from a roaring ocean to a babbling brook. Through it all, I never gave up, although at times Bill and I gave in. Through my efforts to capture the united front, I was tenacious and ever the optimist. Bill learned the benefits of verbally supporting his spouse, making joint decisions, and staying the course.

Do not pass GO, do not collect $200, and do not take your firstborn home from the hospital until you adopt the united we stand position. This parental goal is a must if you want to be in charge of your children, reduce friction with your spouse and your family, and project the appearance of sanity.

Robin G. Banks

* * *

Red roses are common,
Parrot flowers, a rarity.
If you want to parent well,
You must practice solidarity.

CHAPTER TWO

BAGGAGE CLAIM

Recognizing Your Past
and Dealing with It

Taking the occasional weekend off from chauffeuring kids and refereeing squabbles was a must to re-establish my sanity. My mother-friends and I would travel to Myrtle Beach, South Carolina, to relax in the sun and take advantage of various "shopportunities" in the clothing and souvenir shops that were on every block. Our mandatory visits to gift shops often reminded us that our holiday was short-lived. We would momentarily be snapped back to the real world by the assortment of items displaying pithy sayings about our stereotypical lives as mothers.

"Hey, Clara, look at this." I pointed to a shelf of embroidered pillows.

My girlfriend picked up one of the pillows, and then read aloud, "Are we becoming our mothers?"

* * *

As I dealt with my children, I often heard my mother's voice come out of my mouth as if she'd taken up housekeeping inside my head. "I'm only going to tell you one time," I would say, or "Wait till your father gets home." These tired warnings still echo throughout households today and probably will forever.

Not only did I tend to say what my mother had said, I also tended to do what my mother had done when doling out punishment. That's not to imply that the parenting style of the past doesn't have merit. It only demonstrates how deeply embedded it was in my psyche and how easy it was to fall back on the way I'd been brought up.

Your past is over. You can make your own choices now that you're a parent, or better still, before you become one. But first, redirect your course by making informed choices rather than totally relying on your past and how you were raised. However, even though you want to create a new beginning making better choices, ironically you have to return to the past to claim your baggage, and then deal with it.

Discovering and accepting your baggage won't be as thrilling as soaring through the sky in a hot air balloon, but believe me, it will be worth every minute you devote to the process. This journey will strengthen you as a parent, providing insights into why you behave the way you do. Claiming this baggage and working to discard it promise greater success in guiding your children toward healthy lives than if you didn't return to the past as a first step in redirection.

How I Was Reared

I grew up a baby boomer in the age of *Donna Reid, Leave It to Beaver*, and *Father Knows Best*. These television favorites depicted a simpler time when doors were left open, kids peacefully roamed the neighborhood and walked to school, the milkman delivered milk and eggs to your door, moms stayed home, and a family included two parents.

My childhood was just like that. On the negative side, it was a male-dominated world. The father brought home the paycheck, ruled the household, and made all major decisions. My parents' style of parenting was autocratic. They told me what to do and I did it with little chatter. They taught me right from wrong and to respect authority. Back talk resulted in a soap sorbet and being sent to my room.

Mom and Dad expected me to do my best in school and every other part of my life. My mother taught me good manners and instilled in me a love of music. I had house rules: go to bed on time, clean my room, and no sassing. When I became older, I was expected to obey curfew.

My parents chaired school fundraisers, such as barbecue lunches and sweatshirt sales. They were scout leaders and coaches. Mother was my Sunday school teacher. And as long as the Earth rotated on its axis, I attended Sunday school and church every week. Some of the greatest times were church outings to Rankin Lake for covered-dish picnics, softball and dodge ball with the adults, tossing horseshoes, and exploring the creek with friends.

My parents and I had fun together but like many others of their generation, they simply didn't know how to talk to children. Although they participated in my life as leaders, their involvement was more physical than personal. For example, they provided food, shelter, clothing, and transportation but were unaware of any childhood dreams I had. I remember I prayed to grow tall so I could have long legs and audition to be a New York City Rockette. If that fantasy fell through, I would become a member of the Peace Corps, definitely a more realistic possibility than kicking up my legs at Radio Center Music Hall.

I'd wanted to be a writer since junior high. Dawn Larson and Jack Jamison were to be the love interests in my future romance novel. My parents didn't know about that childhood dream, either. Nor did they realize I needed guidance in setting goals and solving problems. Likewise, they didn't understand I had to talk things out before I knew what I thought, so I could decide what I could and would do. It's no wonder my questions and opinions remained in hibernation for so many years. My parents and I didn't talk, which was still the case when my future husband came into my life.

I remember it clearly. Blue sky, eighty degrees, and no humidity. A glorious summer day. The outdoor reception was over, and guests were leaving our home when I slipped away to my parents' bedroom to change into my going-away ensemble.

The room was still, and I could hear the faint good-byes of family friends who lingered in the backyard. The calm surroundings and the rhythmic ticking of the Big Ben clock on the nightstand invited me to sit down for a minute after the day's frantic pace. I flopped down on the corner club chair, my wedding gown billowing out around me. My head eased back onto the cushion. Thoughts of the day filled my mind and a smile found my lips. Barely a minute had passed when I heard the click of the door knob. My eyes sprang open. I raised my head.

"Oh," my mother said. "I didn't know where you were, honey. I want to help you change."

She seemed a bit flustered as she walked in. I jumped up, my reverie gone.

"Could you help me with these buttons?" I asked.

Avoiding eye contact, I noticed she was wringing her hands. *Oh, my gosh, she wants to say something about the wedding night.*

"Mother, I can't undo all these buttons," I said a little louder than I'd intended.

We stood there as my mother undid the zillion, tiny covered buttons. When she finished, I hurriedly removed my going-away outfit from the hanger and began to dress. I would have completed my task more quickly had I not buttoned my blouse one buttonhole off. Mom carefully hung up my gown, smoothed out the wrinkles, and folded and refolded the long mantilla veil until the corners matched perfectly.

After zipping my pants and matching my shoes to the correct feet, I made a beeline for the door. "Thanks!" I called as I strode down the hall.

"Honey, any questions about the wedding night?" Mom ventured, her form filling the doorway.

"No, Mother," I tossed back as I rounded the corner to the den. *What?! The birds and the bees now?*

* * *

In my household, intimate discussions were the exception and not the rule. If my mother had ever broached the subject of sex with anyone, surely she had preceded it with a stiff drink. As it happened, she had partaken of a glass of champagne during the wedding festivities but evidently not enough for her to sit me down to have the sex talk. At sixteen years old, I'd been forced to uncover the pamphlet hidden away in my underwear drawer since the sixth grade to confirm what would happen on the day when I blossomed into a bona fide woman.

Your past doesn't have to be your future. Deciding to do things differently, however, is not enough. You and your husband must keep a dialogue going with your child from the outset. Put him at ease by giving him your undivided attention and time. This relaxed atmosphere opens doors to trust so he can more easily approach you, even with such dreaded topics as puberty and sex.

How I Thought I Would Parent

As a naïve, married woman in my twenties, I told myself: I'm going to be a better parent than my parents were. My youngest son Mark echoes those exact words today. But he goes a step further and says he's not going to parent "in any way, shape, or form" like Bill and I did. When he enters parenthood, I'll be eager to see how long it takes before he has to choke down his unfounded confidence.

Bursting with enthusiastic idealism and seeking a different path from that of my parents, I intended to open lines of communication with my children, spend quality time with them, and explore their deepest thoughts and feelings. With my firstborn, I planned to tweak the past: keep the good and sift out the undesirable to create a parenting style sure to produce fantastic, flawless children. Everything would be just so: perfect children, perfect husband, perfect life. Isn't that what all moms dream about? I wasn't dreaming. I was hallucinating.

Did I know how to rear my baby girl with calm, good humor and a gracious respect for her as an individual with specific and general needs? Did I have a wellspring of memories of personal relationships with my parents from which to draw? Not exactly. Still, there were books on parenting. After looking at a few, I found them far more complex than the clear explanations I needed fast. With nowhere else to go, I reverted to what I knew best: my past, which sat hunkered on the backyard fence like a bird of prey poised to strike.

I was chained to the past and to unreal expectations. Expecting to be the perfect mother, I imposed high performance standards. I believed that everything I did wrong or didn't handle in just the right way would emotionally scar my children for life. My every mistake would irrevocably tarnish their chances of becoming good people and socially acceptable adults. I took myself way too seriously, making the already difficult job of parenting even harder.

Furthermore, my mother or father hadn't asked for my opinions or offered any advice on parenting. Their generation didn't do that. My opinions were crammed inside my brain until the day I dared to launch my first one. I was, after all, a married adult with two children. At thirty-two, standing at my mother's kitchen sink after Sunday lunch, I ventured a personal thought. The fact that I even had one was amazing, if not liberating.

I challenged her opinion of the minister's message that morning. Her surprised reaction as she turned to face me was followed by spasms of coughing and rapidly blinking eyes. Don't remain frozen in the past. Defrost your thoughts and opinions; think and speak for yourself. After all, you're a smart, creative individual who can direct your future with new ideas and ways of doing things.

Preparation

Clearly you can't prepare for everything before your first child. Initially, you might think that because you're madly in love with your dreamy spouse that you already know everything you need to know about him. However, when your baby arrives and your mate begins to interact with the newest family member, certain behaviors and beliefs might surface that will surprise if not disturb you.

If you didn't talk about your emotional baggage before marriage—and I lay odds you didn't—first claim the baggage you brought to the relationship. Open each suitcase with care in the presence of your special someone and note every item that has been packed away. It's not a bad idea to consult a counselor to help you take inventory of your less-than-healthy traits. You can also ask parental advice from someone whose childrearing skills you admire. The sooner you sort out your baggage, the better.

Taking time for introspection into your past and present behaviors as well as looking at what parenting involves can boost your confidence. You'll get a preview of what's to come, and you'll discover tools to help you cope. I'm not talking about a formal plan with Roman numerals. Rather, you should engage in an honest conversation about making good choices and identifying roadblocks that could hinder those choices.

It's great when you can ask the hard questions: Am I a control freak or am I flexible? Am I a perfectionist or can I be satisfied with something less? Do I avoid commitment or do I readily engage? Do I procrastinate or complete tasks in a timely fashion? Am I a pushover or do I stand my ground? These pointed questions are tough to answer, but a yes to any of the negative traits can derail an entire family.

Honest talks with your spouse will help you pinpoint how you feel about religious training, spanking, making rules, underage drinking, parenting as a team, or simply eating dinner together. After coming to terms with these kinds of questions, you can consider your differing behaviors and thoughts on parenting before coming up with a strategy that satisfies both of you. It takes compromise and perseverance to make the choices that most benefit your children.

Surprise complicates the situation. So rather than jumping into parenting and free-falling all the way through it like the generations before you, don't leave to chance the most important job you'll ever undertake. Loosen the chains of the past. Give yourself permission to discover who you are and bone up on what lies ahead. Even a risk-taking skydiver packs a parachute to soften his landing.

Personal Baggage to be Identified and Claimed

I was in my mid-thirties when a behavioral flaw surfaced. I served on a committee of a civic group and a problem arose about scheduling a fundraiser. Rather than hearing out the leader's suggestion, I interrupted to offer my opinion and why it was the best option. In that moment, I discovered a pushy attitude. I returned home troubled.

Ashamed of my bad behavior, I took a good look at myself. Often when matters didn't go my way, I would mutate to a knee-jerk specialist whose self-control evaporated like mist on hot pavement. I didn't think others saw me that way, but I knew that that part of me had to go. Fortunately, my conscience, blaring away like a race track public address system, told me I could change.

Believe it or not, it had never occurred to me before that the way I acted out my frustration was unacceptable. This revelation, wherever it had come from, was a blessing, the seed to my becoming a better person.

Because our firstborn was an easy child to raise, my self-control problem had more to do with my interactions with Bill than with Dede. I tried to change but when we disagreed, I usually fell back into the habit of storming the front lines via a lively presentation of my views. Attila the Hun was on the move. I know I exaggerate when I equate my behavior to the "Scourge of God," but I was upset about what I'd learned about myself. Mortified of my unbecoming behavior and beating myself up for it, I cited Attila the Hun because he was the worst historical figure I could think of. Right or wrong, that's the way I felt back then.

I was angry for two reasons. First, I blamed my parents for allowing me to grow up with a self-control issue. Second, I was angrier still because now I had to invest time in dealing with a problem I believed should never have existed. After the initial flurry of angry feelings, I calmed down. I had a choice: I could deal with the problem or not. I chose to be responsible—who wants to be a jerk?—and tackle it with genuine intention.

Meanwhile, we had a second and third child. The relative tranquility of marriage with one child disappeared. My plans to conquer my limited self-control faded away like sunlight at sunset. But I had made an effort. I had talked with counselors and attended parenting classes, but that was after all three children had arrived. By then I was bouncing off the walls like a silver ball pinging off the bumpers of a pinball machine.

The years went by and before I knew it, I was in my forties. The kids ranged from elementary to high-school age. One afternoon I caught a few minutes of the Oprah Winfrey program, featuring a child psychologist. That's when I first heard the term baggage used in a sense other than luggage. The doctor said everyone had negative feelings and behaviors, which he referred to as baggage. He added that this baggage, formed during childhood, could cause difficulties in adult relationships.

I knew then that I had been lugging around excess baggage picked up in my childhood. Suddenly, I understood the root of my problem with self-control. I had grown up in an environment where practicing self-control wasn't often modeled when things didn't go well. But I didn't have to be permanently flawed and sentenced to bad behavior. I could rewire my past.

The excuse that you can't change is baloney. We all have room for improvement and seeking help is a wise man's decision. But some people don't want to go soul-searching for fear of what they might find. It's easier not to know. Well, this old dog was going to learn a new trick even if it took a whole bag of Kibbles 'n Bits for her retraining. Imitating Bill's calm reserve would be a lofty challenge because reacting without control was so ingrained in my being. I set my determination to the max once again.

Dealing with My Baggage

Until the Oprah Show, I hadn't realized that Bill and I had baggage let alone how important it was to sort it out not only for our well-being but also for our children's. As a mother and full-time laundry technician, I began to look at the idea of emotional baggage like I looked at dirty clothes: they lay in the basket until someone decided to wash them. Now was the time to lighten my load. Before the program, I couldn't figure out why I acted the way I did. Nor could I move toward patience and a united front with Bill until I sorted out my baggage.

My self-control struggle and Bill's desire to operate separately formed an almost impenetrable barrier to teamwork. Until I could get some traction with my problem—disable Attila the Hun—the united front would remain just a wish. Not connecting those two goals delayed any progress Bill and I could have made. Of course, Bill would also need to discard his baggage, his parents' way of doing things, so he could embrace teamwork and sign on the dotted line.

By the time my last child Mark began the ninth grade and Andy entered his senior year, much experience had flowed under the parenting bridge and pooled at my doorstep. I had gained confidence and a better understanding about how I operated and why teens acted the way they did. I had begun to neutralize my self-control baggage with a tactic I had invented. When a situation arose in which I might push the anger button, I had conditioned myself to recite a mantra: Stay cool. Keep it together. Saying those words in my head gave me time to think before I responded.

After several staccato recitations of the mantra, I pressed my tongue against the roof of my mouth. I'm not kidding. This prevented it from flapping around and yielding bad fruit. I then willed myself to listen, listen, listen, even if the emotional intensity of the dialogue escalated. As long as I remembered to plug into the zone created by the mantra, I could choke back any quick decision or judgmental remark that would fuel the fire.

My mantra enjoyed success a time or two with my youngest son's rudeness, the test of all tests. During these bouts between Mark and me, a positive reaction or lack of any reaction on my part always made a productive outcome more likely. And if that wasn't enough to get excited about, my spirits soared when Bill chimed in with: "Mark, don't talk to your mother like that." Ah, how luxurious that plush fur felt as it wrapped around my body.

Rumor has it that I kept my cool when the children reported speeding tickets and dented fenders. By the wide-eyed looks on their faces, I must have thrown them off with the new Mona Lisa Mom. It was a better fit to Bill's Mr. Rogers. Attila the Hun was melting away like the wicked witch in the Wizard of Oz. Reprogramming my software had paid off.

To be honest, I didn't always fare so well. At times, my improved self-control got knocked around and so badly nicked when Mark's rudeness blindsided me that my automatic mantra shut down. I then ran straight to the Auto Zone for ailing bodies to repair the loose wiring. After having my emotional settings tightened, I put my shoulders back with my head up, knowing there was always another day to get it right.

By that time, I had learned from a counselor that beating myself up for losing my temper was a colossal waste of emotion that served no useful purpose. Mentally flogging yourself is one more piece of dirty laundry that should be washed, bleached, and hung out to dry. During the following months, my tenacious pursuit of patience helped me effect a behavioral change, not a total change to be sure, but enough of one to give my spirit an inner peace that before had been lacking.

If you are also a member of the knee-jerk club, you're in good company. I'm sure you can come up with a more lyrical mantra than mine. Actually, any gimmick will do as long as it keeps you from opening your mouth while your brain is in the lock position.

Take comfort in knowing that many people struggle with this problem. It's one thing not to be aware of a behavioral problem; it's another to know about it and do nothing to change it. Switching the channel from a practiced behavior to a new one is tough; it takes sheer willpower and reconditioning through practice. You can see why it's best to recognize and deal with your baggage before you have a kid because if you don't, your spouse and children will provide many opportunities that will expose the stuff you've been carting around and test your control at every turn.

Get off to a good start. Gather your courage to scan your past for baggage and be prepared to admit to it. Committing to the hard work to correct it promises growth in maturity and increased parenting success.

More Baggage to Claim

I remember longing for an emotional connection with my children. Having a good relationship with them would help me unravel who they were, know their thoughts and dreams. To succeed I would have to do things differently than how I had been raised.

But the question I needed to ask myself was how do I go about doing things differently so that I could reach my goal. That question eluded me. Instead, I reacted to my parents' autocratic style of parenting—no personal discussions, mostly directions and demands—by going overboard with my attempts to converse. All three children were in the lower grades at the time. When the three o'clock bell rang and they jumped in the car, I bombarded them with questions: "What did you do in class? Did you go outside for recess? Who was in your project group? Tell me about your new friend."

As youngsters, Dede and Mark were OK with my Spanish Inquisition and answered most of my questions. Andy, however, was not as forthcoming. When he responded, his answers were short and left gaps in the details I thought I needed to build our relationship. To this day, I remember feeling strongly that passing along the baggage of limited conversation was not going to happen in the Banks household.

Years passed with minimal success. Assured by my naiveté that my grown-up teenagers would naturally seek the wisdom of the caring woman who had suffered extreme physical pain to bring them into this world, I persisted with my onslaught of questions, not having a clue that I was going about this project all wrong.

Dede and Mark did share, but by virtue of their admission into teenhood, their good natures had now acquired limits to excessive chit chat. When they thought I overstepped the bounds, they cut me off by using the gesture talk to the hand. Aware of the point and intended humor behind this trendy response, I eventually got the message. I reeled myself in and turned off the recording of questions they'd heard so often that they'd become desensitized to them. A new approach had to be found.

As for Andy the teenager, extracting information from him or merely trying to engage him in conversation was as exhausting as trying to squeeze size ten hips into size four pants with only one percent spandex. Something had to give.

As I delved into the past for an answer, I discovered the critical part timing plays in successful conversations. For example, whenever I asked one or all of the children to sit down for a minute—often without regard for what they had been doing—they knew I was about to launch into one of my mini-speeches. I'm sure I lost them after the first paragraph. That they were stifling yawns or shifting from haunch to haunch escaped me. My voice droned straight through their brains and exited like the sound of a beehive in mourning.

Looking back at the general picture, I concluded that choosing a time that is convenient for both parties—don't let your teen tell you there is no good time--is the first ingredient for a beneficial mother/child interaction. Though it may sound ridiculous, set up a time to have a talk with him, the same as you do with your doctor or business associate. The teen is a hard creature to pin down. If you have to, make an appointment.

The second ingredient to a successful conversation is to adopt an attitude that less is better. Be succinct and specific. Kids don't want to listen—they have their own agendas—to a long drawn out discourse of warnings and dangers. If my kids saw one of these talks brewing, they often gave me a drippy excuse about why they needed to be elsewhere. They might also avoid me altogether as if I was springtime poison ivy. That disappearing strategy went double for my older teens, especially if my favorite "nothing good happens after midnight" topic was on the docket.

Mix these two ingredients and you'll likely get your child's attention and receive a better response from him. Unfortunately, I made my greatest strides with this newly acquired wisdom after the children had left home.

Authentic Conversation

As a young married woman, I was under the misconception that if you could talk you could communicate, that is, talking and communication were synonymous. Furthermore, my belief that communication was as natural as breathing could not have been more wrong. Meaningful communication is a powerful tool, and proficiency in it would be helpful to me in all my relationships. And just as important, I would become a good model of verbal skills that I could pass on to my brood. I needed to be enlightened.

As if my younger sister had been eavesdropping on my thoughts, she called me one afternoon to tell me about a professional seminar she had attended in Texas. She wanted to know if I'd be interested in a cassette if that word doesn't date me, I don't know what does— on communication. What were the chances of that happening at this particular time in my life? I was forty-five years old, my daughter had just entered high school, and I was searching for help.

Dr. Jody Potts, then adjunct professor at Southern Methodist University and head of the consulting firm The Lively Mind, was the speaker. She gave the most on-target explanation I'd ever heard about the moment when real communication takes place: ". . . when the message being sent is the same as the message being received in a oneness of understanding."

I was so awed by that statement that I memorized it. That in itself was a miracle considering that by then much gray matter had been leeched from my brain by my whirl-about family life.

"A oneness of understanding" unlocks the message you want to send or the story you want to tell. That's a simple explanation of a skill that is difficult for many people. Being clear and confirming that everyone shares the same understanding isn't as easy as it seems. So often people don't focus on what's being said. Their minds are racing to corral their own thoughts so therefore they don't engage in real listening. Consequently, they miss important information. Other times they rudely interrupt to insert their own thoughts, which prevents the speaker from finishing.

After pondering the essence of good communication, it dawned on me that sharing your opinions involves more than a verbal exchange. It requires cooperation, which translates to patiently listening as a basic first step to authentic communication. Many times I found myself running past what my child was telling me to get to the bottom line. I wasn't focused on careful listening or understanding. Asking questions or inserting judgmental comments before he finished was unfair and confused the situation as well. He had a right to be heard without interruption and judgment. How could I expect him to be patient and non-judgmental with me if I wasn't willing to do the same for him?

After listening many times to Dr. Pott's tape, I observed other people's discussions and conversations. I also participated in counseling exercises on effective communication. But could I apply what I had learned in real life? If the sun was out, the sky was blue, and my stomach full, then the answer was yes. Note, for example, this conversation with Dede:

"Hi," I said. "Anything interesting happen at school today?"

"Yes, but it's so complicated I don't know where to begin." Dede's face was so long her chin drooped to her toes.

"Would you rather talk about it later?"

"I just don't know why she did that."

"Why don't you start at the beginning?"

"Well, Sally wanted to go together to the game on Friday. I told her I wasn't sure I was going. I said I'd get back to her on Wednesday. I find out today she's going with Jessica. Now I don't have anybody to go with."

"Uh-huh." I nodded.

"I'm really mad at her. She shouldn't have done that. I thought she wanted to go with me."

"Since she asked you, it sounds like she does want to go with you. Did you talk with her later to let her know your plans?"

"Not really. I was working on my project and forgot. And besides, she was absent two days, so I didn't see her at school."

"I bet Sally would love for you to join them. How do you feel about giving her a call? It's going to be a great game and I know you'll have fun."

"Well, maybe . . . I guess so."

* * *

I let Dede be in control when I asked her if she wanted to talk at another time. When she continued, I waited until she had finished airing her feelings before I commented. Making helpful sounds and gestures lets her know I was paying attention. I asked questions at the end to clarify my take on what had been said. We both had to be satisfied that we had reached that oneness of understanding.

Furthermore, I remained neutral by not siding with my daughter. That allowed her to make the final decision. Since she was so disappointed, I refrained from stating the obvious, that she should have called Sally to confirm the outing. She already knew that as well as I did. That successful conversation was a good step toward establishing the emotional bond I so desired.

For many of us, listening with patience takes practice, practice, and more practice. Listening without judgment also requires focus. When we do these things, we demonstrate respectful behavior toward our children. That model is directly related to their self-worth. We also pave the way for openness and trust.

When I took a closer look at myself, I saw that effective communication was more than self-expression. It also hinged on learning to holster my impulsive tongue. If I could do that, I could then replace a knee-jerk specialist with a good listener. I'm certain my teens would have been more comfortable coming to me with their problems had I been a better communicator right from the start.

The Silent Type

On the other hand, sometimes no matter how well you express yourself, your child might not be a talker. Children are as different as DNA strands, and these differences are especially true when it comes to sharing information. Some tell you nothing; others tell you more than enough to short-circuit your grid.

When questioned, some children resort to the "I can't explain it" excuse. They'd rather not be bothered, a popular escape in our household during the teen era. But some kids don't have the confidence or verbal skills to express their feelings and thoughts. I often accepted the "I can't explain it" response when I should have coaxed my child to give it a try, and let him know that I had plenty of time to listen. Self-expression improves with practice, which leads to increased self-confidence and verbal participation.

In reality, you have limited time to teach your kids to effectively communicate during their formative years. During the years before high school, the word "home" evokes images of the family's eating together, the possibility of productive conversation, and laughing at the kitchen table, especially at dinner time. Teens' access to cars and participation in sports and other after-school activities nearly erase that familiar family scene. Don't let your home become a place where your offspring eat an occasional meal or use it as a drive through. Together-time is crucial to healthy emotional development; it strengthens the family core as well as hones verbal skills in a relaxed atmosphere. The family supper table is one part of the past you must keep alive the best you can.

Although finding quality time together was hard, I didn't give up. I continued to push for real conversation. I believed it was a way to be in my children's lives, never realizing that my goal wasn't theirs. Knowing how they felt about dating, drinking, drugs and who their friends were was crucial to being a good parent.

Andy wasn't big on my question-and-answer routine. Our history of verbal exchange was superficial. "I can't explain it" meant he didn't want to be bothered. A counseling workshop helped me to change those scenarios. Instead of firing off questions that prompted minimal responses, I began asking questions that would elicit more thoughtful replies rather than a simple yes or no.

Andy was in his senior year when I began asking, "What do you think?" That seemed like a natural question to ask a child, but it wasn't for me. No one had ever asked me what I thought. I definitely was stuck in the past. One simple question opened the way to mutual respect and trust between us. My oldest son's participation took on a new dimension. What before had often been a one-syllable response progressed to a refreshing, though brief, exchange of ideas. We were on the verge of a meaningful rapport, and it was none too soon since college was on the horizon.

The same thing happened with Andy's brother. Even though Mark didn't hesitate to tell me what he thought, at times with all the accoutrements of a fireworks display, our heated volleys diminished by the time graduation rolled around. We had both matured—somewhat—allowing for a positive bond to be within my grasp.

When Mark moved away to college, it marked the end of a quarter century of children living at home. Not long after his departure, I found myself sitting in a silent den, listening for the faint echoes of prior conversations. The communication skills I had learned helped create more positive verbal exchanges. Still I wondered if I had truly communicated deeply with my children. If I had set my goals too high, my intentions had been honorable, despite the fact that my know-how had been lacking. But a giant step had been taken toward more mature relationships. I was proud of that.

New Lessons

Over the years I've learned that some things require more time to pan out than others. Today the five of us often come together to talk about life and people and how to be better human beings, the very kind of exchanges I had longed for when they lived at home. A blend of patience, openness, and honesty with genuine communication helps solidify an emotional connection with your child.

From the moment our children are born, we parents strive to connect with them through authentic communication. We seek mutual respect and understanding. If we model this to our children as they grow, it will be easier for them to engage us and others in worthwhile conversations. Idealistically, having this ability in place before the children arrive will make the rocky teenage years more bearable for everyone.

Bill and I were untrained, unprepared, and unclear about what parenting entailed. We hadn't unpacked our baggage because we hadn't known we'd had any. Nor did we discuss parenting as a team, being good role models, making rules, disciplining, fostering independence, or spiritual growth. We took for granted that all this would happen and that our children would turn out well.

Likewise, we had no discussions as to whether our children would develop character traits, such as integrity, trustworthiness, kindness, or generosity. Like our parents, we had a tacit understanding that our children's lives would be governed by these principles. And just like them, we didn't know we should talk about how to instill these values in their lives. That was our reality when the stork landed on our doorstep with our first bundle of joy.

There is no audition for parenthood. When you have your precious baby, the job is automatically yours. Obviously, reading about and discussing parenting is not the same as experiencing it. But the good news is that you don't have to walk the same path as many parents did in previous generations. Get straight in your minds how husband and wife can operate effectively. Face the road ahead by being informed and claiming your baggage before you have to wipe runny noses, referee battles, or issue edicts of global concern to rebellious teens.

Get A Grip

* * *

Roses are fragrant,
Orchids, a vision.
Secure your past;
Face the future with decision.

CHAPTER THREE

MONKEY SEE, MONKEY DO
Setting a Good Example

It was lunchtime. The house was quiet except for the toddler squirming in a highchair and smearing peas over his face. His mother, neatly dressed in khaki shorts and a sleeveless, white blouse, moved about the small kitchen with surgical efficiency, preparing lunch and planning the evening supper.

"Mama, more peas, peas, peas, peas, peas," the toddler squealed, laughing at the sound of his voice.

"OK, pea man, give me a sec. I need to find some of Granddaddy's corn for tonight." The young woman blew a wisp of blond hair out of her eyes, turned away from the sink, and headed to the refrigerator.

The freezer was jam-packed with fresh-frozen pint containers of vegetables and fruits her father-in-law had grown in his three-acre garden at the farm. When the mother opened the freezer door, a

65

barrage of bricklike containers crashed to the floor. She jumped back in time to save her bare feet from being hammered. She uttered not one bad word. She smiled, pleased with her agility and verbal control.

"Mama, ya s'pose' to say 'Damn it,'" exclaimed the cherub-faced boy. The woman's smile vanished.

* * *

Confession time: I was that mother and that toddler was Mark. I couldn't believe my ears. I had inadvertently taught my son bad language.

Although I didn't want to make too much of this isolated incident—one little curse word—if I continued to use bad language in front of my child, it would be the first step down the wrong path. Bad language is what I had modeled for him and he had been an excellent student.

From that moment on, I vowed to scrap all four-letter words in my vocabulary. Though I'd been ashamed at the time, and certainly my toddler didn't know what he was saying, today I give him kudos for timing and pronunciation. I have a knack for uncovering a silver lining tucked away in most adversities. It's called survival.

Follow the Leader

When I think of the word "model," I think of something or someone worthy of being copied. Herein lies the glitch: not everything or everyone who is copied is worthy. I've therefore expanded the meaning to include monkey see, monkey do behavior, a behavior in which children mimic others without distinguishing between good and bad.

Even though my toddler's surprising understanding of the situation and what he thought was an appropriate response took place years ago, the lesson I learned then still holds true today: never underestimate children of any age. Just because they are busy talking or playing doesn't mean they aren't tuned in to what you say and do. Their little wheels are always turning and more often than not they will catch you when you least expect it.

Consider, too, that the teenage brain resembles the toddler brain in that both can appear to be on another planet yet zero in on your not-so private remarks. However the teen, unlike the innocent toddler, jumps in at just the precise moment to take advantage of your less-than-perfect behavior. Full of righteous indignation, he then proposes to use this parental oversight as leverage to excuse his own unacceptable behavior. However embarrassing it may be, don't let the clever lad get away with his ploy. Apologize, restate the rule about bad language, and from then on monitor what you say in front of your little darlin's.

I realize this news of monkey see, monkey do behavior won't make the lead story on CNN since its negative practice is commonplace in families throughout the world. Nevertheless, it's a behavior that needs to be talked about and avoided by parents, especially new parents, who are often so focused on going from point a to point b, particularly with their little ones, that they don't think about how they're getting there.

The Banks supper table didn't escape the negative side of the monkey see, monkey do behavior. It was fertile ground where anyone could observe this unrefined conduct more often than I cared to think about. Consider the following example:

"Burrp!" Bill let a loud burp slip out. We had just sat down and finished the blessing when civilized behavior ceased. With lips pursed, I turned my head ever so slightly to glance in his direction, waiting for him to excuse himself. No response.

"Bill," I said under my breath.

"Burrrrrp!" Another belch ripped from the throat of my giggling, teenage daughter. Bill joined in the laughter.

"Dede, stop that!" I said.

"Bill, did you hear your daughter? Beel?" He was no help and obviously enjoying my distress. By now, Dede was doubled over in laughter.

"Burrrrp, burrrrp!" The younger boys, hearing no warning from their dad, demonstrated their own guttural blasts.

Now the chorus included all the zoo animals. The burping had become a contest of who could belch the loudest and the longest. It was four against one.

"Y'all just wait," I said. "One of these days you're gonna embarrass yourselves out in public. You too Bill. I can't wait for that to happen."

Exasperated, I sighed and slumped in resignation. Bill attempted to compose himself and voiced a half-hearted reprimand. The kids laughed even louder. I couldn't blame them. In one breath, their bad manners were applauded; in the next, they were told to stop and not do it again.

My husband's credibility crumbled like a chocolate chip in a baby's fist because he chose to behave poorly. He therefore sounded the bell for our children to do the same thing. And, too, they knew they would suffer no repercussions because their father had led the charge.

Having been married to the man for over fifteen years at that time, I knew he wasn't bothered by this extracurricular activity and that he was merely jerking my chain. I wouldn't have gotten my knickers in such a knot had I been confident that Bill would support me the next time the burp-a-rama erupted. But I knew pigs would never go airborne.

* * *

Children's mimicking bad behavior and parents condoning it is nothing new. I wasn't above laughing at bad behavior but only when it was someone else's child who repeated an off-color remark his parent or another relative had said—grandfathers and uncles were the worst. The laughter died, however, when my child did it.

My embarrassment led to my scolding him when in actuality I was the source of the problem. I was the grown-up, and if I ignored good modeling and disciplining, my child's repeating my words or actions would become a habit. His habit would then become a pattern of behavior that would negatively characterize his personality. The innocent child doesn't understand why he is marked as obnoxious, crude, or ill-mannered. He becomes an outcast, and he hasn't even begun kindergarten.

This leap from laughter to outcast might seem dramatic, but the negative cycle can lead to disruptive behavior, difficulty in relationships, even to depression. Eventually, this downward spiral can give way to dangerous behaviors, such as drugs and alcohol use or the emotional and physical abuse of others. Like all those undesirable things that float around our lives—bad manners, disrespect, drugs, alcohol, etc.—they are taken much more to heart when they're in our own living room.

Children live what they see and hear. They observe us just as we observed our parents. I remember my mother remarking about how unattractive she was. Because everyone commented on how much I looked like her, I grew up thinking I was unattractive. Little did she know how this innocent comment would affect me throughout my life. Accepting a compliment has been and continues to be awkward for me to this day.

We don't realize how much our actions and our comments about ourselves and others affect our children. If we complain, our children grow up discontented, never satisfied. If we criticize ourselves and others based on physical appearance (weight, hair, facial qualities) or abilities or anything else, we pass on destructive self-criticism and a judgmental nature. Children are watching and learning even though what we say and do seems harmless and trivial.

But modeling is two-sided. When we demonstrate love and empathy, we instill in our little ones the art of nurture and the act of caring. When we can say I'm sorry and tell the truth, we demonstrate humility and integrity that children fold into their characters. These examples represent only a token sampling of the extent to which we influence our precious charges, so we must be on guard to reflect all that is positive and good.

I want my adult children to know now what I didn't know then: when you decide to have a family, you must make a conscious decision to set a good example by talking with your mate about questionable behavior, so you both can come to acceptable terms about how to deal with it. You do this from the beginning, because your behavior is monitored from the moment you bring your baby home. Each one is a feeling human being, a little sponge of good and the not so good.

Setting a Good Example 24/7

To think parents can be on their p's and q's all day long is unrealistic. It just ain't gonna happen. Occasional lapses are normal. Everyone loses control, makes mistakes, or responds to a situation with a knee-jerk reaction. One memorable trip to the mall with my three kids, ages ten and under, still leaves me red-faced today.

"May I help you?" the sales clerk asked.

"Well, actually, I would like a cash refund," I said.

"Do you have a receipt?

"No." I placed the makeup on the counter. "This eye base is dried up. It's no good."

"Ma'am, I must have a receipt to give you cash back. I'm really sor—"

"I thought these products were guaran—"

"Mama, come on," Mark whispered, growing antsy.

"Ma'am, they are guaranteed. I can give you a gift card and you can buy a new one." The clerk's politeness never wavered.

"I don't want a gift card. I'd rather have the money." I wasn't going to be sidetracked with a lesser offer. Besides, it was the principle of the thing. By that time, Mark was jerking my sleeve. I bent down to deal with him, while the clerk rang up the gift card.

"I'm sorry for the problem," she said. "You may use this card on any item in the store."

Now all three kids were tugging on my purse, ready to run to the closest exit. I realized I wasn't going to win this battle and reluctantly took the card. "Thank you."

The cordial response was ingrained in my being even though I was irritated. I grabbed a child's hand and turned to leave, but not before I said, "This is ridiculous." I was determined to have the last word, even in defeat. Looking back, I may have been the adult, but I had acted like a child.

Once home, Mark exited the car, catching up to me as I climbed the stairs to the back door. "Mama," he called, getting me to turn around on the landing, "your voice sounded mean when you talked to that lady at the mall." He might not have had a pencil in his hand, but he had been taking notes all the same.

Gathering courage from her little brother's remark, Dede added, "You were a little rude."

I stopped so quickly I almost flew out of my shoes. It was normal for me to scold them for misbehaving, but they had turned the tables on me. I had not gone postal at the cosmetic counter, but I had been rude. Mark probably didn't understand exactly what had gone on, but Dede did. She called me on my sub-par behavior, for which I was grateful.

"I'm sorry I wasn't nice and embarrassed you," I said. "I was wrong." I had been sideswiped by my children and needed to regain my footing.

* * *

Being remorseful and admitting that I'd mishandled the situation showed them I didn't allow stubborn pride to interfere with what was right. I was modeling honesty and humility. Young children, in particular, are more likely to forgive you, accept you, and listen to you when you've been honest and apologetic. In turn, the trust you display by showing them you can be truthful sets a precedent for a better relationship with them in their teenage years. And believe me, you'll need everything in your arsenal to cope during those demanding days.

I didn't know it at the time—the scene at the cosmetic counter happened pre-Oprah—but I was living out the baggage from my childhood when immediate reaction trumped listening. My impatience, accentuated by my abruptness and the desire to drive a hard bargain, set a bad example. I wasn't happy being a prisoner of this unbecoming, behavioral habit that could emerge at the slightest prompting. In the future, with my baggage tidied up, I would take the lead in setting a good example by treating everyone with courtesy and respect, the way I would like to be treated.

Even if you don't have a self-control issue, you'll occasionally slip. You'll have a bad day. The kids will have bickered nonstop or hubby will have forgotten to pick up the dry cleaning with the dress you wanted to wear for the next day's school luncheon or you'll have remembered too late that hard-to-reschedule doctor's appointment. You're human, trying to keep your feet firmly planted while living in an overly stimulated state of existence. And when you're having one of those human days, talk with your children openly and explain your actions. Be accountable.

Realistically, I know that practicing what you preach all the time will happen only when children stop asking for money. And, too, every family has that certain behavior that becomes part of the family lore; that is, that funny, off color stuff you share, laugh about, and reserve for family consumption only. There can be a fine line between being uptight and anal and being practical and forgiving. Use your common sense. And like everything else in life, do your best. Set practical goals, such as being a good role model. Keep them top priority through weekly check-ins with your spouse, or whatever works best in your household, and exercise prudence and consistency in carrying them out.

Do As I Say and Do As I Do

Parents often yield to "Do as I say and not as I do" to excuse their lazy behavior. This adage is nothing more than an inside-out message of diversion. Adults use this phrase because they can; they are the parents and sit at the top of the power pyramid.

Children need someone to look up to, someone they trust in word and deed. If adults preach one thing and do another, they send kids the wrong signal: adults are exempt from the rules. A parent must practice what he teaches in order to get his message through to the kids. The popular adage then becomes "Do as I say and do as I do." Don't confuse your children with mixed messages.

My husband relied on the "Do as I say and not as I do" instruction every Friday night when we motored to a nearby restaurant. Dede was fourteen years old, Andy ten, and Mark eight. We climbed into the blue and white minivan, children in back, Mama in the passenger's seat.

"Seatbelts buckled?" I asked.

Bill started the motor, and then put the car in reverse. As he backed out, deftly maneuvering the wheel with his left hand, he popped the top of his after-work libation with his right. The process was a choreographed dance with each step occurring in the same sequence every Friday night.

"Bill, you cannot drink and drive," I whispered through gritted teeth. And so began my weekly campaign for setting a good example.

"We're less than two miles away," he said. "I'm fine."

Several Fridays later, Bill came up with a plan that would not deny him his liquid pleasure. Once again we piled into the van and assumed our places. Bill placed his red Solo cup in the cup holder between the captain's chairs.

"Do you really think the kids don't know what's in that cup?" I said. At that time the word "idiot" was still a part of my vocabulary. Even if I didn't voice it that night, it was beating down the door of my cerebral cortex.

"They can't see through the cup," he said. "They're not even paying attention."

"The kids aren't dummies."

About that time snickers burst forth from the back of the van.

"Hey, Dad, what's in the cup?" Mark and his brother weren't going to let their dad get away with what he thought was a foolproof scheme for disguising his beer.

"Iced tea, Son."

Laughter exploded from the rear of the van. I turned to face Bill. He was chuckling; I was not.

* * *

Even though the mood was light, except in my cloudy corner of the van, the message to the kids was serious: adults get to make the rules but don't have to follow them. I was angry and frustrated that he wouldn't listen to me. I feared the kids would think that drinking and driving, even a short distance, was all right.

I never could change his mind. However, now with stiffer punishments for breaking the law and the reality of how much heartache results from driving under the influence, I shiver to think how costly it could have been to our family and anyone else on the road. Trust me: it's much easier to follow the rules when the rule-maker sets a good example.

The Children's Take on the Friday Night Ritual

I assumed the message back then had been obvious to the kids. But while writing this book, I decided to email them to check on the accuracy of that assumption. Dede said that because she had never seen her father tipsy, much less drunk, she hadn't thought much about his drinking and driving. Andy's memory was vague, but he didn't think drinking and driving was wrong. He added that his dad's Friday night routine didn't affect him one way or the other.

Mark's memory was clear. The boy may have his shortcomings, but his mind is razor sharp when it comes to childhood events. He knew something wasn't right. It happened that the Banks Friday night ritual coincided with the weekly Drug Abuse Resistance Education (D.A.R.E.) program that Mark's second grade class was participating in. During one of those sessions, the policeman leading the presentation declared that drinking and driving was illegal. Mark's hand instantly shot up to confess that his dad drank and drove. We could always count on Marky boy to tell it like it was, an exemplary young man in sharing all things Banks.

The teacher, who was a personal friend, thought our son's public disclosure was funny and called to share it with us. However, the officer's response was not so humorous. After class, he gave Mark his card and told him that if he ever needed anything, he could give him a call. The reality of parents habitually modeling bad behavior can smack them in the face when their young children innocently expose them, and can do so when they least expect it.

Bill didn't have his Friday beer at home because we wanted to arrive early at a popular restaurant, so we wouldn't have to wait in line with three active children. For me, keeping my threesome in line for more than fifteen minutes was as stressful as trying to get my husband to ask for directions on a trip—men are not from Venus, that's for sure. In the final analysis, neither Bill nor I was willing to change our habits and compromise for the good of the children. Once again, not acceptable.

During recent years, we've laughed a lot about Mark's broadcasting his father's drinking and driving to the entire second grade. At the time I thought Bill had lost credibility with the kids, which he hadn't. Nor did his weekly beer at the wheel ever resurface as leverage to justify drinking and driving when our kids became teenagers. Their silence contradicted everything I'd heard about kids using every bit of ammunition to get their way. Perhaps our children had been too young to recognize the danger. To the disappointment of the second-grade teachers, the D.A.R.E. program hadn't gotten through to Andy and Dede, at least, as far as their understanding that it was illegal to drink and drive.

Even so, when in doubt, practice what you preach and behave the way you want your kids to behave. With children more is caught than taught, and you never know what will stick and what won't.

Teen Years and the Trickle-down Effect

While raising three children, I noticed that imitating undesirable behavior was not exclusive to the very young. Basking in the glow of having received her driving permit, my fifteen-year-old daughter was cruising down the road in the family auto when another driver to our right rolled through a stop sign at the intersection. He then made a left turn in front of us.

"You idiot! I can't believe that guy." Dede's eyes never left the other driver until he passed her.

"Dede!" I cried.

"Well, he pulled right out in front of me."

"He probably didn't see you."

"Mom, he's an idiot. He didn't even look."

Thank goodness it hadn't been a close call, because my daughter had been attentive and slowed down. I was however more concerned with her language than with the other driver's carelessness. I immediately recognized myself (and my mother) in her tone of voice and in what she'd called the other driver. From our lips to hers. I hadn't thought one second about the consequences of my road language.

* * *

That scene triggered a memory from my childhood. My mother, a person who never used improper language, had nevertheless created a legacy by using the word "idiot." Using the alternative *id'git* would have softened, to some degree, the word's crudeness, but history reveals that both my mother and I favored the unbecoming version over the slang.

The word took on a new coarseness when blurted from Dede's innocent lips. Name-calling and impatience while driving were stepping stones to road rage. She was surprised when I explained that she had learned that unladylike word from me. I apologized and promised myself to curb my language and be a more tolerant driver. I achieved that goal quickly because no mom wants her kid going around calling everybody idiots.

To rectify the negative side of monkey see, monkey do, honesty and setting a better example is the best policy. Don't ignore your part in modeling the bad behavior nor try to defend yourself. Instead, admit your fault and work together for change.

The Positive Side of Monkey See, Monkey Do Behavior

The positive side of monkey see, monkey do is as pleasing as the negative side is displeasing. After the name-calling incident, I decided to practice at least one good deed a day while driving:

"Mom, why are you letting all those cars go in front of us?" Dede asked from the backseat.

It had become my habit that when waiting in slow traffic, I would allow several stopped cars on my right to merge into the line ahead of me. "I'm trying to be a courteous driver. Someday I'll want somebody to let me in. Besides, what's the rush? It's only a couple of seconds." I wanted to put patience up there with cleanliness.

And speaking of driving manners, it used to jack my wires when another driver slid into a parking spot I'd obviously been waiting on. But was it worth my anger to get all bent out of shape about it . . . in front of the kids? I shouldn't have allowed anyone to get to me like that. It was up to me to take control. That was a lesson I had to learn and learn fast.

In the beginning of my retraining, I learned to let most of my anger go, even if another driver was making me nuts. I didn't say a word. However, I did feel the need to slice up the other driver momentarily with my razor sharp stare. I felt better, afterwards. Hey, I'm human. Today I've progressed to the point where I don't react with any anger or take that sidelong glance. I stay calm, though I might succumb to the urge to make a humorous remark. Better that response than risk a full blown a-fib attack.

Yielding to the other driver and not letting him upset you set a good example for the kids. It isn't a matter of winning; rather, it's about resetting your emotions for the good of the kids, and for yourself as well.

If you're an attentive observer, life can offer teachable moments wherever you go. During one of our many memorable trips to the mall, the children and I witnessed a shouting match and an exchange of finger gestures when two people vied for the same parking place. You would have thought it was a NASCAR event with drivers competing for the pole position. It looked as if the two drivers were going to ram one another.

Since actions speak louder than words, the children learned a valuable lesson: being a jackass could be hazardous to your health, or your car. It's only a parking place, not worth wasting one drop of precious energy on some road-enraged ding-dong. Today all three children practice the one-good-deed-a-day driving rule. I know this because I've seen their courtesy and patience many times.

Be What You Want Your Children To Be

Like our parents, Bill and I were ordinary people wanting to do the right thing despite often being sidetracked by our humanness. We weren't predisposed to think about positive role modeling, and consequently we didn't consider the effect everything we said and did had on our children. I operated at a whirlwind pace trying to get housework done, meals prepared, errands run, and children groomed and dressed without giving much thought as to how I behaved while doing those tasks.

As parents, you guide and direct your children. You help them form their identities. They learn a sense of honor, respect, compassion, spirituality, even a sense of humor, and so much more by observing how you speak, act, and react. If you want to have children with character and integrity, you must first display those traits yourselves. If you want your children to prosper as human beings and in their relationships, check your own reflection in the mirror.

Everyone has established habits and patterns of behavior that may or may not be beneficial to pass on to children. Your investment of time and energy in preparing for parenthood can offer you a better chance to deal with those undesirable habits and patterns before you start your family. When you do your homework, sacrificing what you'd rather be doing, to become a better role model, you grow to be an example of everything good you want to gift your children.

Should they marry and have families, they will have at their disposal, sealed in their memories and ingrained in their characters, the sound principles and positive behavior they saw modeled at home. And so a new cycle begins. Your children advance one giant step forward in the process of preparing for healthy parenthood and family life.

* * *

Roses are red,
Violets are blue.
You'd better do right
'Cause someone's watching you.

CHAPTER FOUR

THE ART OF MAKING RULES
Do's and Don'ts

Torrents of water snaked down the den windows in dirty rivulets. This would be the only washing they'd get this summer. The house was dark except for the lights in the kitchen and the soft glow coming from a lamp in the den. The periodic lightning filled the windows with fleeting shadows. As the storm gathered momentum, the thunder got closer and louder. The three young children scurried to the den to huddle with their favorite toys. They were getting along nicely until the boys did what boys do after having been cooped up all day.

"Leave my stuff alone, Butt Brain," Andy said as he jerked Colonel Slaughter, his GI Joe Green Beret, from Mark's hand.

"You're a butt brain," Mark hollered back. "Mama, Andy hit me in the mouth. I wudn't doin' nothin'!"

83

"Mark, come here." I was sitting at the breakfast table sipping my afternoon glass of iced tea. "Turn your head . . . not too bad. Rinse your mouth with cold water and you'll be fine."

With a hug, I sent him off to the bathroom. Meanwhile, Andy and Dede had begun squabbling.

"Andy, it was your fault. Mark was just looking at your guy," Dede said.

"He broke my Joe. You're just a Dede peepee, a big fart face."

I entered the den in time to catch that last brotherly endearment. "OK, enough with the name-calling. What's going on, Andy?"

"Mark grabbed my GI Joe and pulled his arm off."

"You did it when you grabbed him from me," Mark said, running back into the den.

"Enough!" I said. "Your brother has a bloody lip, Andy. Do you know how he got it?"

"Andy did it," Dede offered. "And he called me bad—"

"It wasn't my fault," Andy said. "He ran into my hand."

"For heaven's sake," I said. "What's the rule?"

"No hitting, but I couldn't help it."

"And no name-calling, right?"

* * *

Not until I rewound the film of my life as a mom did I realize that rule-making is more than reeling off a list of do's and don'ts. It's an art form. Granted, it's not on the same level as glassblowing, but it still requires time, talent, and creativity.

If I could do it all over again, I would ask myself four questions when setting rules:

- Who makes the rules?
- What's the purpose of the rule?
- How many are needed?
- How are the rules stated?

Origin of the Banks Family Rules

When I fell in love with Bill, I thought I had felt and known all there was to feel and know about love. Within the security of this blissful emotion, time and worry ceased to exist. Then I gave birth to Dede and learned the meaning of unconditional love. Looking into the wrinkly, red face of our wailing new bundle, I knew I'd tapped into the outer realm of the divine, God's hand in the flesh. Soaring headlong through waves of wonder, I knew I would always love this child, no matter what.

Our first creation weighed in at nine pounds fourteen ounces with a cry that sent engineers of earplugs back to their benches. Despite the eardrum crushing cries, she filled Bill and me with anticipation. How exhilarating it would be to be in charge. We would make the rules. We would make the decisions. We would make everything.

Then a realization hit us like an arctic dip: the responsibility for this tiny being rested entirely on our shoulders. Our euphoria evaporated like steam from a sidewalk vent as we discovered we didn't know anything about rearing children and that there wasn't much time to study. So we humbly tucked our ignorance into our pockets and turned to what was familiar. Like generations before us, we had only the past for our guide.

Like a tadpole in a jar of water, our firstborn grew up and started hopping around. She quickly turned into a little person with a mind of her own. Based on my childhood experience and an article I had read in *Parents Magazine*, while waiting at the pediatrician's office, I knew Bill and I should set boundaries. These would give our daughter a sense of security as well as a sense of right and wrong.

Children need to fit in. Whether they realize it or not, they want rules like everybody else. Rules exist everywhere: at the workplace, school, church, recreational arenas, roadways, malls, parks, restaurants, anywhere you go. The sooner children accept the need for rules, the sooner they will belong, equipped with a boost of confidence and on the right path to playing nice in this world.

Who Makes the Rules?

There's more to making rules than saying whatever rolls off your tongue when your child does something he shouldn't do or doesn't do something he should. After having read the first chapter, you've guessed that both parents should make the rules together regardless of who stays at home and who works. Even though I desperately wanted Bill and me to parent as a team, I practiced selective teamwork when it came to rulemaking.

Since I spent more time with the kids, I made an unconscious decision to set down most of the rules without giving any thought to including Bill. What a gift it would have been to have had his input. My decisions in settling disputes or refereeing wrestling matches would have carried more clout with the kids had they known Dad had a part in making the rules. Then they would have better understood that they would have had to answer to both of us.

Setting limits together helps to more peacefully and effectively manage the household. There should be no doubt in your mind at this point in your reading that mom and dad should operate as one. Eliminating confusion about who's in charge gets everyone off to a solid start.

What's the Purpose of a Rule?
How Many are Needed?

A rule should exist for a reason. It might be for personal safety, guidance in daily living, or parental sanity. The rule must be fair and reasonable. I would be surprised if you've never overheard an exasperated mom saturating her two- or three-year-old with instructions such as these: "You promised Mommy you would sit down and be still. Keep your hands off your brother and be quiet. You know those are the rules when we eat out, young lady."

While having a purpose for each rule is important, expecting a preschooler to obey that stream of demands indicates overmedication or having suffered a blow to the head from an errant boomerang. A young child isn't able to process three or four instructions at a time. He can't handle a long list of rules that govern every little thing you want him to do or not to do. Neither can the parent effectively oversee such a long list. In effect, if you have a rule but don't honor it, then you don't have a rule.

The first step is to prioritize and limit your rules. Include only those that require immediate attention and that correspond to a particular time in a child's development. The second step is to give your child time to adapt to a rule. Consistent obedience to rules comes with maturity. Your child will learn about life and will develop character by the gradual implementation of rules. This process of maturing through obedience will be cumulative.

How is a Rule Stated?

Being a Spanish teacher and curious about language, I enjoyed advancing the kids' verbal skills by using new words and expressions. After the scene with the name-calling, I let the boys know their language was *inappropriate*. Well, that term went right over their heads. I quickly recognized from their blank expressions that getting the rules understood took priority over my vocabulary enrichment program.

Wording of a rule requires thoughtful consideration if you want to have a oneness of understanding with your offspring. Needless to say finding the right words and including only enough detail so as not to bore the child is indeed challenging.

After a quick shuffle of the deck, I elaborated on the name-calling and no hitting rules for their benefit:

"Listen up. Butthead, butt brain, and fart blossom are off limits. What would your friends think if I called their dads fart face or butt breath?" Convulsions of laughter erupted as they fell to the floor, beating their fists on the rug. "That kind of talk makes you look like you were brought up in a cage. Do you understand, Andy? Do you understand, Mark? Do you understand, Dede? I included her to cover all my bases.

I'm convinced boys come down the chute hot-wired for less than genteel language. We moms must stop them early on before colorful language becomes a habit.

"OK. We have a new no-hitting rule too. No hitting means no punching, swatting, kicking or pushing in the nose or the mouth, in the head, the shoulders, the legs, the butt, or anywhere else on the body for any reason, even if the other person started it."

To make my point, I gently pushed, kicked, and hit. Wanting to be totally specific and avoid any loophole some clever child might find, I went a step further.

"Is everybody listening? The rule also means you cannot hit your brother or sister when you're in the car, in the yard, in the grocery store, in church, on the sidewalk, or at restaurant. Does everyone understand? No hitting any time, any place. That goes for hair-pulling, too." While I had their attention, I sneaked that one in for Dede. Sooner or later, that would be the boy's natural progression in physical contact.

Because I explained the rule in terms they related to and improved the rule by adding details, the kids and I came to an understanding (of sorts). There were fewer incidents of hand-to-hand combat and less bloodshed.

I not only wanted to be clear and specific with the children, I also believed I should present the rules in a respectful tone of voice. After spending time in the hot zone of refereeing clashes from the normal to the ridiculous, I discovered that my kids were more likely to accept the rules when I used a calm voice than when I spoke out of frustration or anger. Showing respect is rewarded with respect.

I now know that being too general, like our first no hitting rule, which was concise but neither clear nor specific, will leave the door open to lame excuses

To insure your kids get the message, I offer one more suggestion. Have them explain the rule back to you in their own words. This will give you the chance to clarify any misunderstandings and therefore prevent mindless excuses like I couldn't help it; it's not my fault, you started it; you didn't say that, I thought you meant something else; or

I didn't know." They'll use these favored expressions to get around any rule and to deflect all accusations of guilt.

A Rule for Personal Safety

After you've conquered the art of rulemaking, figure out a good place to start when setting up the house rules. In the early years of our household, rules that kept our family safe and provided our home with reasonable order and good mental health were first on the agenda.

Bill and I knew that situations or behavior dangerous to life and limb had top priority. One of our first rules when the children were old enough to toddle around was no playing in the street. When Dede was still too young to understand the rule, she wandered into the road in front of our house.

Luckily, I caught her before a car came along. Whisking her back onto the grass, I knelt in front of her, and looking her straight in the eyes with my hands on her shoulders, I sternly said, "danger danger," the two words that I would later repeat anytime there were circumstances that could cause bodily harm. I then popped her once on the palm of the hand to make sure I had her attention. Her pitiful face and streaming tears rattled my heart, but the pop on the hand worked.

Later I talked to her about how the big cars could hurt her just like Daddy did when he'd playfully wrestled her to the ground, bumping her head on the hard floor. She likely understood the consequence for breaking a rule before she understood the reason behind it. I'm sure she didn't associate the word "danger" with a life-threatening situation, but with a minor hurt like a pop on the bottom or the palm of the hand. My little pleaser understood she had done something wrong and never ran into the street again.

Then Andy arrived. He became my two-year-old *extraordinaire*. Under the illusion that he would obey me as Dede had done when he, too, strayed into the road, I was surprised when he didn't. I followed the same procedure with him as I had done with his sister. I whisked him out of harm's way. I then knelt in the grass in front of him, and placing my hands on his wiggling shoulders and looking him square in the eyes, I repeated the words danger, danger, and then popped him twice on the behind. He wasn't fazed in the least. Before I could turn around, he was back in the street, his chubby legs churning fast ahead of me.

Off I went down the road with arms flailing like a warped windmill. When I caught up with him, I scooped up the squealing scamp, who undoubtedly thought he was playing a fun catch-me-if-you-can game. There's no reasoning with some miniature people, especially one who is having a marvelous time.

That scene repeated itself several more times with the same ending each time. Cement and Andy's head had a lot in common. Finally, I issued an edict that all of us would stay inside until he got the message that he couldn't use the road as his private playground.

At that time Dede was still too young to play outside without a playmate. Though she was upset and thought it unfair that she was being unjustly punished, the situation worked out. Without any hesitation, she let her little brother know exactly how she felt: "It's all you fault. You won't listen."

Maybe Andy felt sibling pressure, maybe not. But I do know that he loved to play outside, so if he wanted to ride his Big Wheel, toss the ball, and play in the playhouse, he had to obey the rule. After several boring days inside the house, subject to his sister's unrelenting complaints, he got the message, and we returned to the great outdoors.

A Rule for Personal Sanity

As a wiser parent today, I understand that issues that irritate you the most require a rule if only to prevent premature baldness. Dede was seven, Andy was almost four, and Mark was sixteen months when we moved into our new house. I felt like the Pied Piper; everywhere I went, they followed. I must have spent a lot of time in the bathroom because G.I. Joes, Little People, baby dolls, and books littered the floor. The builder assured me he had indeed put in a tile floor, but I couldn't see it under the carpet of toys.

Every time I stepped on a Tonka truck or smashed in the face of a favorite doll, I would yell, "Put your toys where they belong or else!"

Sometimes I would follow up on the "or else" and sometimes not. I was going nuts with stuff spread out all over the place. My yelling and threatening did nothing to clean up the mess in my bathroom. What I needed was to attack the source of the problem rather than the symptoms.

The rules we had at the old house apparently never made it onto the moving van. A change of residence is a big deal for children. They needed time to adjust from their old one-level home to their new two-story one. At some point during the endless weeks of unpacking and getting our house into shape—an experience I hope never to repeat—I stopped long enough to think through the problem.

I found our old toy basket in the attic and placed it in the empty den where there was more room to play and no furniture yet to straighten up or damage. I had a powwow with the kids and explained that I had returned to the old house to retrieve the rules. If they wanted to play with their toys the following day, they were to put them in the basket before bedtime each evening. If they didn't, I would put the toys away for several days.

To be successful, I monitored the process. When telling them what to do bombed, I got down on my hands and knees beside them to toss action figures, stuffed animals, miniature vehicles, and whatnot into the basket. Toddler Mark received a free pass, though I did walk him through the motions. When I converted the chore into a basketball game with points scored, he joined his siblings in the fun. Confiscation of a toy now and then, along with a reminder to clean up, reinforced the rule.

Once your kids are safe and you can clear a path from room to room, rules for respecting personal property and bedtime naturally follow.

Respecting Personal Property

After the GI Joe incident between Mark and Andy, I saw a need for a rule related to personal property. I explained the rule in a calm way, being specific yet brief.

"You may play only with your own stuff," I said. "If you want to use your brother's race cars, Joes, Ninja Turtles, or anything else that doesn't belong to you, you must first ask him. If he is not home, then you can't play with his toys."

The children were clear on the new rule. After that, there were very few squabbles regarding property rights. They respected one another's things and were good about sharing, particularly if they woke up liking each other.

Dede had no problems with the boys' wanting to borrow her baby dolls, tea sets, and other girly things. She was three and a half years older than Andy and six years older than Mark, so she saw her brothers as, if not quite her own personal property, at least, available and convenient.

Preschooler Mark became one of her most prized school students along with Baby Huggums and the Care Bears. He was agreeable to anything she asked, including being outfitted in her dresses, ribbons, and bows. It seemed that both brothers came in handy as live dolls. Their availability for dressing up and playing school was Dede's unstated rule. Lucky for her, Andy enjoyed the activity as much as his brother did.

Bedtime

Dede's baby book indicates that she began sleeping through the night within eight weeks of her birth. Andy's baby book is not as kind. He was six months old before he began sleeping all night long. Since number two child didn't require as much sleep as his sister, number three knew he had to be good. He gave Mama her much-needed rest very soon after his arrival.

Dede was eight years old, Andy five, and Mark two when I decreed an eight-o'clock bedtime. I thought I might have problems with everyone going to bed at the same time, but the older children rarely mentioned wanting to stay up longer than their two-year-old brother. I was content with eight o'clock and had the rest of the night before me. Believe it or not, those peaceful evenings lasted until Dede went to junior high. Andy's and her bedtime then changed to 9:30, and Mark's, an hour earlier.

Mark's initial reaction was to protest on the grounds of unfair treatment. I convinced him that little boys required more sleep so they could "grow big muscles and be strong." Since he already showed signs of being a rational thinker, he was satisfied with my creative thinking. I didn't know what I had done to deserve such an easy time of it, but deserve it I did.

When the children were especially good, I allowed changes in the nightly routine for televised sports events. Bill, Dede, and I were loyal North Carolina State University fans. We sparred enthusiastically with the two boys who, because they'd been dropped on their heads by an uncle during infancy, cheered for the University of North Carolina. We also made exceptions for children's programs like *A Charlie Brown Christmas* and educational shows. A tad of flexibility and a dash of compromise went a long way in creating a healthy atmosphere and guaranteeing compliance with bedtime.

Praise for Obedience

Making rules and enforcing them was a fulltime job when the kids were little. At times, I was so caught up in the do's and don'ts that I missed opportunities to praise how good my kids were.

Kids like and need compliments as much as anybody. They are more likely to be consistent in their obedience when you appreciate their efforts. What a relief it was not to have to go through that nightly struggle to get them to bed or to nag them to get up in the mornings. I took their obedience for granted when I should have praised them for their cooperation. That was a mistake, and one you can avoid.

On those days when they couldn't do right for doing wrong, I could have been more inventive. I might have given them a verbal honorable mention for standing nicely without getting into anyone's space. Remembering to compliment the kids is a rule I should have made and been more attentive to. It was a positive stroke that would have encouraged their willingness to obey.

Transition to Teen Years

The early rules set boundaries within the family unit and provided order, if only for short periods of time. One moment there would be peace and the next, chaos and confusion would reign; that's the nature of kids. But the rules were reinstated and new ones added as we went along. With each new one, I heard complaining sighs or noisy objections. After several days of strict enforcement, though, the sighs and objections subsided or were lost in mumbled responses.

With Dede's entrance to high school, the structure in the Banks household abruptly changed. Bill and I were in unfamiliar territory and soon found ourselves trading in the old rule book for a new one. We applied the new rules to each child as they entered high school.

Even though the TV experiment had been aborted early on due to a lack of a united front, I revised the dust-covered rule. The teenagers were allowed to watch TV as long as they had finished their homework. Eventually that rule was thrown out because Mark proved successful in balancing his school work with his TV consumption.

Bedtimes were also eliminated as long as the kids got up on time. This wasn't a problem because at some point, all three had begun using alarm clocks. I might have yelled a time or two up the stairs, but I never had to drag them out of bed. The stage was set for a new parenting phase.

Understanding the Teenager (An Attempt)

As you've learned, all three children in the beginning had the same rules to ensure their personal safety, to teach them how to get along with one another and others, and to instill in them respect for others and for personal property. They had household rules, such as no lying on the furniture with sweaty bodies or no snacking without cleaning the kitchen or no entering the house with muddy shoes. There were rules for bedtime, brushing teeth, and other similar routines.

Those rules were all well and good. However, little did Bill and I know how different our firstborn, Dede, would be from her two brothers, who would have an impressive history of mischievous activities during their childhood. When it was time to go to high school, Dede wouldn't require the same set of rules to guide her that our boys would need. And because Dede wouldn't pose any serious problems for us during her three years in upper school, we therefore didn't know what forces needed to be marshaled to prepare ourselves for the boys' entrance into senior high.

While reflecting on those high school years, I began to ponder the teenager, wondering what characteristic it was that gave them their mystique. For years professionals have researched and dissected that age group, hoping to figure out that confusing breed, especially the male member. I did my own in-house research and discovered a little-known secret: raising boys is not like raising children. They are an alien species from a distant galaxy. Some couples produce only girls and are therefore not privy to that essential tidbit. They are shortchanged in their parenting experience because they never have to cope with this intriguing male entity.

Whenever I heard someone relate an escapade involving a boy, old or young, invariably someone in the group would say "Boys will be boys" to explain their questionable actions. Being the mother of two male offspring, I concluded that this explanation originates in the Y-chromosome phenomenon, an unknown quantity that to this day defies reason. To give girls their due, there are accounts of females exhibiting a similar bent toward mischief, which I attribute to a random chromosomal mutation where the X blurs with the Y.

The Y Chromosome in Action

The neighborhood Council of Women—that would be my friend Marge and I—had dealt with the Y-chromosome phenomenon from the time our sons were in knee pants. One afternoon during a neighborly chat, Marge and I concluded that by the time our adventurous lads had reached high school, they had been the guilty parties in a long list of mischief. The events ranged from throwing dirt clods at passing cars to setting off smoke bombs on neighbors' porches. Marge and I hadn't fathomed that rules were required to deter these activities simply because we never guessed our boys would partake in those kinds of amusement. "Duh" would be an appropriate word to utter here.

Another favorite diversion was the backyard camp-out, which clearly required a don't-leave-the-yard rule. My fellow council member's yard backed up to a wooded area and was the chosen place to pitch a tent. Andy, Marge's only son Greg, and another friend said they enjoyed spending the night under the stars, listening to crickets, and drinking in the sweet, fresh air of summer. Hogwash. Those boys were up to something, and we were going to find out. Marge was on high alert.

Their camping escapades were many, but the one that created the most alarm and set jaws to flapping was the time the trio played a late-night trick on a fellow classmate, who lived in the neighborhood. Knowing that Greg's mother, a night owl, would make one last pass before going to bed around one o'clock, the boys each left an extra pair of old sneakers lined up outside the tent. Seeing the shoes and convinced that she heard them breathing, Marge didn't unzip the flap to peek in. She assumed—cardinal mistake—the boys were asleep inside. They were anything but.

Marge went to bed. Meanwhile, the hooligans were on the prowl. Dressed in army camouflage, the boys slinked down the street to Katy's house. With his two friends keeping watch, Andy crept up the steps of her back deck, tiptoed over to the den door, and eased it open. He glimpsed his classmate sitting on the couch watching TV. Cracking the door a little more for a better look, he wasn't prepared for the betraying squeak or the subsequent terrified scream, as evidenced by his nearly falling down the patio steps during his hasty retreat.

The three guys, their hearts pounding like a fleeing victim in a horror movie, raced back to Greg's house. They scrambled into the safety of the tent with no one the wiser.

The next morning Marge called to tell me about the ruckus that had police cars screeching to a stop in front of the Lewis's house. Their sirens had interrupted the tranquility of our cozy little neighborhood. Evidently, I had slept through the excitement.

It wasn't until she mentioned the shadowy figures in army clothes that we simultaneously blurted out, "Do you think . . .?" Where had they gone during all those other camp-outs? No question, the Y chromosome was hard at work in the Hearthstone neighborhood. Lord, have mercy! Boys will be boys.

* * *

The Y factor was the source of much frustration. It was also the very factor I celebrated. The Banks boys were all boy, never a boring moment when they were around. It was not for me to solve the male mystery but to love my guys unconditionally, with a case of Extra Strength Tylenol tucked away in my bedroom closet and a list of specific rules designed to keep a tight rein on the unpredictable Y-chromosome phenomenon.

Driving Rules: Dede

Before we knew it, Dede was off to high school. She had reached a milestone in which driving was the teen's ultimate goal. Being our first child, she became the guinea pig for everything unfamiliar we faced. The driving permit and the license were accompanied by rules from the Banks DMV. As for the permit, Bill and I agreed that she should drive every day in order to become proficient in all kinds of weather. The rule held for all three children.

After passing the written test, Dede received her driver's permit. After school, I would park in the long line of cars at the junior high. Once at the front of the line, I would jump down from our minivan and scurry around to the passenger's side so Dede could drive us home. Even when she complained of a headache or of being tired, behind the wheel she went. On those days the boys, whom I had already picked up from elementary school, complained of frayed nerves and demanded that I call a cab for them.

Finally, July 8, circled in red on the calendar, rolled around. It was the summer before Dede's sophomore year. We arrived at the DMV to join the line waiting outside the locked doors. She passed the road test and eagerly drove us home, then immediately backed down the driveway to go solo. She embraced her new skill with confidence. She was free to drive to school, to church, to her friends' homes, and to the mall. Not until the end of the tenth grade did we allow her to drive forty minutes away to Charlotte for shopping, dining, and movies.

Driving Rules: Andy and Mark

At first, it made sense that the boys would have the same driving rules as Dede. However, it soon became apparent that the rules had to be customized for each child. Adjustments were made according to their maturity level and, truthfully, the shape I was in by the time the last child reached the upper halls of learning.

From the beginning, Andy was an excellent driver. Finding no reason to object, our tailored rule allowed him to go out of town a month or so after receiving his license in the tenth grade. By the time Mark was eligible, a new state law permitted driving up to 9:00 in the evening for the first six months.

When I heard that, I would have said ten Hail Marys, but I was Methodist and had only a strand of pearls. Instead, I thanked God for the legislature's infinite wisdom, particularly since Mark's tendency was to hug the center line. My shattered nerves were evidenced by the passenger's side carpet having been rubbed bare from my ineffective braking. Outside of several speeding tickets and a few crumpled fenders, all three children did well. Though we didn't condone the tickets or enjoy the hike in insurance premiums, we were fortunate that no one was ever hurt.

Respecting Others: Inappropriate Language

Respecting one's parents might not have been an officially stated rule, but the children knew Bill and I demanded their respect in word and deed. I went beyond policing their grammar to subjecting them to my lecture series on disrespectful and inappropriate language.

One of my problems was that Bill didn't flinch when our sons made off-color remarks or used four-letter words. I, on the other hand, was quick to point them out as disrespectful. Bill, being subject to the Y-chromosome phenomenon himself, believed the guys were kidding or merely trying to get a rise out of me.

It was The Boys' Club and our guys loved being members. Even if they were joking, they said things that shouldn't be said in front of their sister or me. I could jest with the best and laugh at bathroom humor like everybody else, but I wanted my boys to know when to put on the brakes, especially in front of the fairer sex.

With Bill on the boys' side, my leverage to correct their remarks almost disappeared. Still, I continued my campaign to bring up ladies and gentlemen. Those so-called lectures I mentioned weren't confined to just my sons. I bent Bill's ear a time or two, informing him that how our children acted at home was a dress rehearsal for how they would act in public. When he mulled over that perspective, he soon realized the error of his ways and began to scrutinize our sons' verbal choices.

Getting children to heel, as it were, has become an increasingly difficult job due to a more permissive society that condones disrespectful language as well as crude behavior. Respect for self and others doesn't allow excuses or compromises, regardless of what "everybody" else is doing. My children would know what was acceptable and unacceptable based on a standard no different from that of my parents' generation—cursing and sassing were grave infractions that were simply not tolerated. This standard of behavior demanded total respect for authority, a respect that has all but disappeared in much of today's younger population.

Because I kept the rule active and cautioned the boys, their dad included, today I notice positive results. They clam up when I come into the room if they're telling X-rated jokes or using language I don't like. They're not perfect and have occasional lapses, but I excuse those after a brief warning, because they are making an effort to do the right thing.

Respecting Others: Rudeness

Along with offensive humor and slips with curse words, rudeness became a major concern when Mark reached high school. Before that I'd had no particular problem with either Dede's or Andy's language. I'm bringing up Mark's rudeness again for two reasons: one, to underscore that respecting parents is a core rule that teaches children to respect other people's worth; and two, to explain the root of my youngest son's confusion about what he could and couldn't say to Bill and me.

After much thought about Mark's history of disrespectful comments, I traced his backtalk and rudeness to his preschool days. He'd been no more than four when from the back seat of the van he said, "You don't know everything."

What left an impression was not so much the sass—which was indeed upsetting—but his refusal to accept his language as impolite. I know he listened to my explanation because I could sense his brain crackling from the intensity on his face. After considering the matter, at least as much as a four-year-old could weigh a subject of this importance, he remained firm that he hadn't said anything wrong.

Although I was convinced he wasn't too young to understand, his stubbornness suggested I wasn't getting through to him. That bothered me. Though I didn't have an answer, mother's instinct told me he wasn't trying to manipulate me. That would come later when he was much older and wiser. Not knowing what else to say, I cautioned him again and sent him to his room when we returned home.

The incidents of disrespect during the elementary school years were so rare I placed little importance on them. However, I remained puzzled that Mark wouldn't accept my explanations. Because his junior-high years passed virtually sass-free—an unbelievable achievement—I thought his sporadic rudeness in the earlier years had been a tic-like occurrence he had outgrown. But he and I should have talked more about his reasoning. We did not. That was a huge mistake.

Part of the problem was that Bill and I didn't agree on the occasions when Mark crossed the line. Mark was therefore unable to grasp when his language took a wrong turn. Had we joined forces to give him a clear definition of disrespectful words, tone, and body language, we all would have had an easier time of it. But we didn't. As a result, Bill and I were in for many unpleasant and disappointing moments when our son entered high school. All of us, including Mark, suffered the consequences.

Rudeness Resurfaces

When Mark entered high school, he emerged stereotypically as the source of all knowledge in the free world. He predated Google as a search engine. He knew everything and was never wrong. The minor disrespect of his younger years resurfaced as a major issue, specifically during his senior year. His lack of respect during our conversations alarmed me. One minute he was a delight, and the next he was a donkey's behind.

"Hey, Mom, do you need help with those groceries?" he asked.

"That would be great. Thanks." I popped open the trunk. "I can't believe that Jim guy was stopped by the police last night for drinking in the school parking lot during the game. I thought he had more sense than that.

"Look, Mom. You don't know anything about what's going on today." Mark jumped down my throat without warning.

"How can you say that? I was a teenager once."

"Aw, come on. You've been sheltered all your life. You don't have a clue." His sarcasm stained the garage walls.

"You're out of line!" I had no idea why he had gotten so riled up.

"Well, I'm telling you the truth and I'm right. You need to know that people you don't think drink drink. Drugs are everywhere. You don't know anything."

"Mark, you're being rude when you tell me I don't know anything and especially when you use that arrogant tone of voice. It's disrespectful. I need you to lower your voice and listen to what I'm saying." *Where is the duct tape when I need it?*

"Well, you don't know what kids are doing. All you had to worry about when you were growing up was breaking curfew and smoking."

"Just because I didn't grow up with drugs doesn't mean I don't know they're in your school, that you know people taking them."

"Get serious."

* * *

Despite his comments and his sarcasm, which had my blood boiling, I whipped out my self-control mantra. Luckily, that overrode my urge to flog him or to respond in kind. My attempts to explain the nature of his rudeness to him were no more successful than they had been when he was a preschooler.

I sent him to his room to think about his impolite language and behavior, praying he would someday get the fact that he had been rude. It's unbelievable that it took so long to convince Bill to join the campaign against our son's rudeness, but this incident and Mark's obvious misbehavior did it.

Discovery: Rudeness versus Truth

Unfortunately, I didn't always whip out my mantra in time. I clearly remember one occasion when our exchange so quickly escalated to a volcanic eruption that my mantra was buried under the lava of volatile emotion. Neither one of us listened to the other; my self-restraint vanished like water through a sieve. At one point he shouted, "I should be able to say anything to you, Mom, as long as it's the truth."

The truth part sounded reasonable, but blurting it out did not. Then I remembered an incident that had happened to Mark in elementary school.

"Class, your test will cover everything but chapters two and four," Mrs. Brooks said.

"So we don't have to study anything in those chapters?" Mark wanted to be sure he understood.

"No, just the material we went over today."

Mark and his classmates took the test the following day.

"Mom, I know I'm going to get a bad grade on the social studies test," he said. "Mrs. Brooks put some stuff on it she promised wouldn't be there. Everybody's mad."

"When you go to class tomorrow, why don't you explain to her why everyone is upset and why the grades are so low? If you just tell the truth, I'm sure she'll understand."

* * *

Evidently, I hadn't made it clear that he needed to be polite and tactful while telling the truth. Could his high-school slips into disrespect be the result of my incomplete advice? I spent his senior year trying to convince him that there was a right and wrong way to speak the truth and that he had a choice. He was certainly old enough to know the difference.

Bill and I told him many times that because we were older with more life experience, he should trust us. We ended the discussion by saying that if he chose to maintain his position, then his continued rudeness would handicap his future relationships. It would also keep him in a state of simmering anger that would ignite anytime we broached a topic on which we disagreed. We again relegated Mark to his quarters for meditation.

Progress Peeks through the Clouds

Being the last child, Mark was the greatest recipient of my patience and self-control. In return, he learned to simmer down a little when we disagreed. Sometimes my youngest and I made it through an entire conversation without wanting to throw the other off an I-85 bridge. The air got sweeter, the atmosphere healthier. Bill, Mark, and I made an effort to understand and respect one another.

We've had many similar talks with Mark since those high school days. We told him we were trying to help when we pointed out that his being right didn't make it OK for him to be blunt or arrogant. We tried to get across to him that being wrong in approach undermined any facts he may have been able to enumerate.

The last few years have seen an improvement in how Mark phrases his thoughts. He's less confrontational, which allows for a more conversational tone. Nonetheless, he has much work yet to do. Maturity is as individual as the person. But I'm pleased he is trying to do better, which is all I can ask of him.

The New Golden Rule

When repeating the rules became tiresome for everyone, I adopted a friend's golden rule for teens: do right. It provides blanket instruction for all situations from manners and respectful behavior to decision-making and how to treat others.

I went a step further and advised my kids to ask themselves one question before making a big decision that might go against our rules: Will I be able to fall asleep tonight, or will my conscience butt in to keep me awake? Being a mother and an optimist, I hoped they would listen to that still, small voice, despite the Y-factor and the ever-present peer pressure. The do-right rule is still in effect today.

I can't emphasize enough that making sensible rules that children can follow requires thoughtful consideration. Despite everything families have in common, each one is unique. Some are quiet and reserved; others are lively and demonstrative. Some are structured and others are laid back. Different rules will fit different kinds of families.

Regardless of the family's nature, children need rules. They set boundaries and provide the first guidelines for positive behavior.

* * *

Roses proclaim love,
Although flawed by thorns.
Rules, though tough,
Promote good form.

CHAPTER FIVE

BEHAVIOR MANAGEMENT
Accountability and Discipline

The boys and I had just finished a typical lunch of hotdogs, chips, and the hated beverage milk when I announced that naptime would start in thirty minutes. I wanted both boys to be rested by the time we picked up Dede at a friend's house.

Soon it was time for them to lie down. I scooped up my toddler and took him to the back bedroom to rock and sing to him. I enjoyed the routine as much as he did. After five or ten minutes, I lay my little angel in the crib without a peep from him. My three-year-old was in the living room playing war with his action figures.

"Son, your turn. Mark's already asleep."

"Uh-uh. I'm not sleepy," Andy said without looking up.

When I bent over to scoop him up, he wriggled out of my arms. I then swooped down on him—sound effects included—and picked up a squirming mass of arms and legs. Once inside his bedroom, I stuffed him between the Ninja Turtle sheets. After delivering a firm warning and threatening him with my famous raised eyebrow, I turned around to leave. I had barely passed under the threshold of the doorway, when I heard the thump. I grabbed him around his middle and forced him back under the covers.

"Don't move or else." I was on the verge of losing it.

I closed the door and hotfooted it to the living room couch where I fantasized about taking my own nap. Clearly I was delusional.

Whoosh! Andy rounded the corner to the living room like a tornado blowing through town. I gathered up his flailing limbs amidst protests that he wasn't sleepy. I returned him to bed. He wasn't happy and I was three steps into angry. This scenario repeated itself until I shook his shoulders so vigorously that I rattled his teeth. I must have frightened him, because he finally stayed put. Not a proud moment for me.

* * *

I didn't look for a different solution to Andy's naptime. He didn't require as much rest as his brother or his sister, who'd always taken a nap after lunch when she'd been his age. I was trapped in the box of thinking that what was good for one was good for the other. I should have looked at each child individually and customized naptimes for each one. Playing in the living room while I stretched out on the couch would have allowed Andy some quiet time, prevented our frustration, and eliminated my anger.

No one wakes up one morning saying: I know how to parent. I have all the answers. The job doesn't work like that. Unless and until we make an intentional effort to learn how to be an effective parent, we will likely parent our children the way we were parented, and that includes the bad along with the good.

Generally speaking, I followed my parents' example and punished my children for bad behavior, and I didn't reward them for good behavior. I operated out of a mindset that everything had to be my way without considering other options. I may have thought I was the boss, but often I was not in charge, especially when I was being manipulated by one of the boys. This control attitude often resulted in frustration and resentment when I smothered my teenage son's desire to be heard.

As an individual and a parent, I often questioned how I handled certain situations. Guilt was something I became used to, especially if I'd punished one of the children when I'd been angry. I struggled with this guilt over time and finally found help years later when I attended a parenting program. The program gave me insight into how to teach my sons and daughter right from wrong as well as how to become a good model in the discipline arena.

Counseling Enlightenment

One of the speakers was a child psychologist. He pointed out that punishment was more about stopping bad behavior temporarily than changing it permanently. He used terms like consequences, accountability, and discipline, words that shed a new light on dealing with misbehavior.

A child should understand that he is responsible for his actions (accountability) and that there is a price to pay for bad choices (consequences). Discipline, unlike punishment, is a positive measure that teaches in a constructive way. Discipline changes bad behavior to good by informing and building up rather than tearing down.

Understanding the difference between discipline and punishment helped me discard the baggage of a punishment mentality. Punishment conjured up negative images from my childhood, so why would I want to pass that on to my kids? From then on, when I disciplined, I did it out of love and respect. I focused on the privilege it was to have and rear children.

I strove to be fair and respectful. By allowing my child to keep his dignity, it was easier for him to want to change an undesirable behavior. These significant differences in motivation and result make so much sense. Teaching children in a nurturing way means they grow up in an environment that promotes self-respect and respect for others. This is one basic truth I can pass on with the hope that when my children start their families, they will discipline rather than punish.

Nip It in the Bud

From the beginning, I knew it was natural for kids to want limits; it was also natural for them to test those limits. It wasn't enough to have a rule in place and think problem solved. Children need to learn from the get-go that every broken rule or misbehavior calls for a consequence.

For example, your one-year-old child intentionally moves a picture on the wall that he knows is off-limits because you've warned him several times not to touch it. While he's pushing the picture to the side with his finger, he's watching you to see what you'll do. You're being tested by a one-year-old no less. Stop what you're doing at the precise moment of disobedience and take action without delay. I can't emphasize this enough. Applying immediate consequences without nagging him first to "please stop" or "don't do that again" is crucial to nipping the bad behavior in the bud. Be resolute in your decision so as not to blur the boundaries of who's boss. A pop on the hand or the bottom gets his attention fast and lets him know that he's crossed the line and that you're not going to allow him to get away with disobedience.

You may go round and round with a strong-willed child, but each time he's disobedient, repeat the consequence. And each time after you've made him accountable, put him on your lap, and in a loving but firm tone, refresh his memory that the picture is off-limits. Though he may be too young to fully grasp the meaning of your words, your tone of voice will convey the message. And don't even think about negotiating with him. That would be like trying to talk a frog out of catching flies for supper.

When the child is young, discipline must be immediate. The saying "You reap what you sow" is never truer than when dealing with children. Tantrums that don't get diffused and unattended disobedience in the early years translate into serious rebellion and loss of control in the pre-teen and teenage years. By then, everyone will be miserable, the young person's self-respect will have atrophied, and his maturity and the potential for a respectful relationship with his parents will have reached a dead end.

Rules and enforced consequences are like a pair of socks; you can't have one without the other and achieve the desired result. Everyone is accountable and that means the parent as well as the child. When we parents keep promising consequences "next time," we feel better because we don't want to be the meany, but we send the child a bad message. He doesn't have to respect us. Consequently, he suffers in the long run. He pays the price for our temporary comfort because he doesn't develop the tools or learn the lessons he'll need to negotiate life's relationships and difficult situations.

Parental accountability is paramount if we want to teach our children right from wrong and demonstrate proper behavior. We make them responsible for their misbehavior and bad choices when we follow through on consequences, without being wishy-washy. Parenting is also about self-sacrifice, allowing yourself to be interrupted and inconvenienced for the greater good, that is, helping your children become well-adjusted adults. Because you reap what you sow, tend your garden well; your harvest will be bountiful.

A Return to Punishment

During my childhood my parents popped, spanked, and sent my siblings and me to our rooms. Occasionally my brother and I felt the sting of Mother's dual-purpose fly swatter until the day the rubber part flew off when she clobbered a brass lamp my brother was using as a shield. Humorous though the scene was, my brother and I were relieved at the demise of the flyswatter and its sting on the back of our legs.

Bill and I also popped, spanked, and sent our children to their rooms. One day my childhood family maid Mable, a deacon in her church, saw me popping the kids. She suggested that the hand should be used for love and not spanking. That made sense. Recalling the unreliability of the flyswatter, I put a wooden spoon in my purse during outings. When I caught the kiddies running in the aisles or crawling under the clothes racks at the mall, I did exactly what I had warned them I would do: I gave them a whack on their butts or bare legs with the spoon.

This alternative ceased shortly after its adoption when two blue-haired women witnessed the "abuse" and shot me down with pointed stares. Embarrassed, I returned home and used the spoon for what it was intended, so much for the wisdom of my elders. I dusted off my hands and returned to what I knew best: the past.

Spanking

Bill and I returned to our roots when we spanked our boys with a belt. We hadn't made a mutual decision to do so; we had both been spanked by our fathers with a leather belt. We were chained to the past without considering that we could do something different. It was as if we were on automatic pilot. Our fathers probably felt the same way. When Andy reached the upper elementary grades, I made Bill chairman of belt spankings. Even though he didn't like it any more than I did, he delivered most of them.

While I don't have a problem with a pop on the hand or a swat on the backside, I truly regret having used a belt for punishment, even though it happened only four or five times. During my childhood, the belt was a means to punish through fear and physical pain. This so-called corrective measure accomplished nothing as far as teaching a positive lesson. Yes, I changed my behavior, but it was out of fear rather than understanding. And because I was forced to succumb to the desired behavior my father demanded, I was not only afraid but angry as well. Years later after having reared my children, I recognized this cycle of generational punishment and understood that my parents were chained to the past just like Bill and I had been when we used a leather belt on our boys.

My parents rarely explained why I was being punished. They didn't know they needed to, like so many of their generation. Their comments were mostly limited to "You shouldn't hit your brother" or "I told you not to do that again or "You heard me." However, Bill did something our parents never did. Before the spanking, he talked with our child about the reason for the spanking. After he used the belt once, sometimes twice, on the buttocks, he kissed and hugged him for a long time, which he did as much for himself as for the child.

Because belt spankings were emotionally painful for everyone and physically painful for the boys and because they did little to change bad behavior, we had the good sense to stop them before they caused any damaging aftereffects. We learned there was a more constructive way to get their attention.

Although history tends to repeat itself as it did in our case, Bill and I let the kids know how much we regretted the punishment. By advising them that this extreme measure did more harm than good, we believe that we have stopped this cycle of generational punishment, at least with our children.

* * *

Although I would do things differently now, I have made peace with the past. The belt spankings, which give me shivers to this day, did however produce a positive effect in one area: they charged up the boys' creativity. When our adult sons talk about their childhoods, they often recall a funny story about their resourcefulness when they expected any kind of spanking. This anecdote keeps my promise to you about being honest in relating the good, the bad, the ugly . . . and the funny.

When the boys were around six and nine, they were huge fans of the Ninja Turtle cartoons and movies. The ninjas were oversized turtles that stood upright and practiced martial arts. Growing tired of their plastic version of the ancient, Far Eastern weapons called nunchucks, Andy and Mark moved to metal Chinese stars. When thrown, the stars could poke out an eye, scar the furniture, or put a hole in the floor. Upon witnessing the boys launch the projectiles at one another, I shrieked at them, then jet-propelled both junior ninjas to their rooms to think about the mother of all spankings.

Fear and anger competed for my attention. My imagination went into overdrive, dreaming up ghoulish nightmares, such as a child with two black holes for eyes, wandering around New York City's back alleys begging for food stamps; or a child disfigured for life, a six inch scar angled down his cheek, starring in a TV reality show called *Plastic Surgery Mishaps*.

Clamping my hand to my meager chest—Dolly Parton had it all over me—to keep my heart from ripping through my shirt, I retrieved the metal star that had stuck into the wooden floor. Taking the stairs two at a time, I ordered the boys into the hallway to explain the bodily damage the Chinese stars could have done. I then proceeded to wallop Mark on the backside. Andy received two wallops because he was older and should have known better.

My palm hummed with pain. I couldn't figure out why. Years later, the boys told me they had placed Mark's soft-cover Bernstein Bears books inside four pairs of Spiderman briefs to cushion the blow. Their dramatic cries of pain had been Oscar-worthy. No wonder they preferred my spankings to Bill's.

Bedroom Restriction

When I wasn't spanking the kids, I was forever sending them to their rooms. What was I thinking? That was like tossing Br'er Rabbit into the briar patch. Their rooms were centers of fun and games. Dede played with her dolls and made crafts. The boys sneaked into each other's rooms, raced Matchbox cars, warred with GI Joes, and had imaginary wrestling matches, starring the indomitable Ultimate Warrior.

I could hear their chatter and battle sounds, of course, but I didn't care about all the fun they were having. In that moment, cleaning the house and getting them out from underfoot was a higher priority than teaching them a lesson. Too late I realized my house would always be there for me to clean. The kids however would one day leave, their formative years gone forever.

On the other hand, sending kids to their rooms could be productive if they wanted to be elsewhere. I remember the time my preschooler was playing outside when he defied me. I ushered Mark to his room. From his window, he could hear the laughter of the neighborhood gang that had gathered in our yard. He was upset. So was I. When I closed the door, I heard him grab and twist the knob. Determined to win the struggle, I held the door shut while he tugged. I didn't care how long it lasted; I was going to be the victor even if it meant spending the night in the hallway.

Nobody learned anything that day except that I was stronger and more stubborn than a four-year-old. The ordeal frustrated both of us. Sending Mark to his room would have been more effective had I first taken time for a cleansing breath. Then I could have sat down with him eyeball to eyeball to explain why I was sending him to his room. Since that episode, I've heard that whispering is more successful in getting a child's attention than yelling. Try it, you'll be pleased.

If I had taken those simple steps, Mark would have been in a better frame of mind to accept and understand the punishment. I wouldn't have become part of a battle of the wills. As it turned out, I also suffered for his bad choice. Years later a counselor advised me never to make decisions when upset or to dole out consequences that inconvenience me.

A Senior Moment

When I was in my early forties and the children were in elementary and junior high school, I reached a new benchmark in the aging process one afternoon. That day I abused the punishment of sending the kids to their rooms. It must have been a good day for group misbehavior in church because I sent all three to their rooms for an hour, after we returned home from Sunday lunch with the grandparents. Their plans with friends would have to wait.

Hours passed and I heard neither a chirp nor a holler from upstairs. Finally, Dede bravely ventured a few steps into the hallway to ask permission to come out. Oops. I had forgotten about them. First, I blamed my lapse on God. After all, it was His day of rest, and I too had taken a well-deserved snooze on the couch. Then I apologized to the kids and humbly accepted their good-natured scolding. Whenever I'm forgetful today, they take pleasure in resuscitating this incident, especially if there's a crowd around to entertain with tales of mom's mental deficiencies.

A Handy Deterrent

Somewhere between the spankings and sending the children to their rooms, I squeezed in another corrective measure. On several occasions I squirted liquid hand soap into the young boys' mouths to clean out their dirty words. I can remember my mother doing the same thing to me, but with a bar of Ivory soap. In some circles today that old-timey method of punishment could be seen as going overboard. All I know is that threatening to use the soap bottle resulted in immediate compliance to rule number three: no foul language.

A New Technique

Boredom is a proven technique for disciplining young children. The absence of activity is like watching a snowy picture on TV without sound. Imagine your five-year-old sitting in a chair in the utility room or any other boring place where he could be monitored with minimal inconvenience. When I discovered this tool, it was too late to get any mileage out of it with my first two kids.

I didn't know the technique had a name until I heard another mom call it time-out. Mark, on his first day of kindergarten, christened the term when the teacher called to say he'd been placed outside the classroom for name-calling. I didn't see that much wrong with calling a classmate Vance the Pants, but the teacher knew best. Mark couldn't stand being away from his friends with nothing to do, so the name-calling stopped. I never received another call from that teacher.

I thanked the mother who suggested this disciplinary measure and bought an egg timer (avocado green to match the kitchen décor) to keep track of how long the child was out of commission. No longer was I subject to the repeated question, "How much more time?" or "Can I get up now?" I put the timer where Mark could see it but not reach it.

I usually put him near the kitchen or utility room where I practically lived. When he got antsy and jumped up too soon, I returned him to the chair and added more minutes. At the sound of the ding, he had permission to return to circulation only after I had explained again why he'd been in the chair. This was a most effective tool for Mark. I'm certain it would have been useless with Andy, the boy whose motor refused to shift into neutral.

Being creative fulltime was a pleasant daydream. When it happened, it was refreshing. Using time-out to motivate Mark to remove his muddy shoes at the backdoor or wash his hands before supper worked well. When he was a kindergartener, I put three to five minutes on the timer. As he got older, I added more time. Eventually, he outgrew time-out. I then turned to other methods of discipline, specifically not allowing him to watch a favorite TV program or to spend the night with a buddy.

No, No, No!

When Andy ran out into the road after being warned and then popped on the hand, you recall that the children and I stayed inside for several days. If we had continued to go outside, nothing less than chaining my son to the carport would have worked. I pushed that thought from my mind not because the neighbors might get upset but because the car would be at risk with my imaginative little one tied down so close to it.

Just as "no, no, no" did nothing to stop Andy from using the road as his private race track, the words produced few results for other moms running their errands. I heard mothers say it a thousand times in answer to a request, and a thousand times they relented. I add the empty triple-no to my parental don't list because it invariably results in the child's deafness to anything you say.

Dede was pre-school age when a friend of mine complained about how much she dreaded going to the grocery store with her kids. She spent the whole time saying no as they dumped their favorite candy and sugar-coated cereals into the cart. I pictured her cute little ones piling up as much loot as they could. I also imagined my friend taking more food out of the basket than she was putting in. That was scary.

To begin with, I don't like grocery stores and they don't like me. The supermarket gremlin is always rearranging the food on the aisles, or from aisle to aisle, or eliminating my favorite products altogether. If I had to choose between going to the grocery store or having bypass surgery, I would say, "Crank up the saw, doc!" With three kids in tow, I didn't have time to explore. All I wanted to do back then was to get in and get out. And after listening to that mother and considering my own allergy to food shopping, I needed a plan.

Because Dede posed no stressful problems for me during our grocery store visits, devising a plan wasn't as urgent as I'd thought. She generally behaved and was satisfied with her free sugar cookie. With the boys, I had to lay down ground rules and consequences before leaving home. There would be no begging for food or wholesale dumping of items into the cart. Before leaving, I took orders for Lunchables, favorite cereals, and snacks. There would be no running, no pushing or touching one another, and no wandering off. Was this mission impossible?

They were kids and kids beg. They quickly learned that no meant no when it came to non-essential food items like junk food not on the grocery list. So far, so good. However, I wasn't above bribing them into good behavior if the outing wasn't going according to plan. A sugar cookie often worked. If they pooh-poohed that, I dangled a Golden Book or pack of M&M's before them. Obviously, I didn't want them to expect a book or any other treat every time we went to the store, so I had to limit the bribes.

Some days, under the spell of a full moon from the night before, no amount of preparation would prevent misbehavior. I'll long remember the time Andy used the aisle as a Slip-N-Slide. When he knocked over the entire shelf of Libby's Vienna Sausages—my favorite source of saturated fat—he pushed my launch button. I hopped over the rolling cans and cornered my maniac at the macaroni. I abandoned the buggy, which represented thirty minutes of service to the family, grabbed his arm, and marched the crew out the front door, Andy's feet skimming the floor.

There were several other times when we left the grocery store on the fly. Each time I had to dig deep for the strength to leave that grocery cart and its precious cargo behind. It killed my soul to know I would have to return to that horrid place and start from scratch. Solitary shoe shopping was much more civilized than grocery shopping with three kids.

Once home, I sent the guilty party to his room, which seemed like the right thing to do since I hadn't yet been apprised of the time-out tool. Depending on the fragility of my mental health at having left behind the buggy of groceries, I might also unplug the TV for the evening. That sent the wee offender into a rising litany of, "I'm sorry. I won't do it again. I promise. I promise." Sometimes that punishment ensured a more tranquil visit to the grocery store the next outing; other times, it had no effect, in which case I was at the mercy of the grocery store gods.

Looking back at my boys' antics in the grocery store, I'm amazed that I wasn't emotionally scarred by those outings and that no traumatic events occurred. It was always a plus in my book if no blood was shed or bones broken.

The pep talk at home helped eliminate much of the irritation of grocery shopping with three kids. And although I boast of a good record of staying firm with my no, I assure you that, at times, I gave in like the rest of parental humanity.

Financial Charges

During the writing of this book, I would call or email the children to verify information about one incident or another. It was during one of those conversations that Dede reminded me I had fined her and the boys for each rule infraction or misbehavior when she'd been in junior high. I did remember, but thought I had successfully repressed that dark period of insanity. Initially, I charged everyone a quarter, and then later raised the fine to a dollar. The practice wasn't something I did regularly. When I was in a mood, meaning I'd had it, I would charge them for anything they did wrong, from calling each other names to forgetting to feed the dog.

Mark said it was worse than that. He recalled that during those charging sprees, they could be fined for nothing more than looking at me the wrong way. That could very well be true since the income received during the reign of money-gouging was lucrative enough to support my Krispy Kreme habit. Nothing like a glazed raspberry-filled donut to help you forget your cares while satisfying your sugar addiction.

The boys, not being the pleaser Dede was, were frequently separated from the money they'd accumulated from allowances, birthdays, and Christmas gifts. The pain was clearly visible on their faces each time they withdrew coins from their private stashes. I thought that since I hit them where it hurt having to pay fines would be a deterrent to misbehavior. That wasn't the case. It was merely an exercise in collecting money.

For one thing, the basic premise was flawed. The money belonged to the kids and it wasn't mine to take away. For another, it was unfair to charge fines sporadically and without warning. Fortunately, the charging binges died a natural death after a very short run. That so-called strategy might very well be classified as the lamest initiative ever, though I might find partial justification of my actions by falling back on the saying, "Desperate measures for desperate times."

High School

Teenagers come up with great ideas all the time, but they don't think much beyond the ideas. Their teenage brains want what they want when they want it and are therefore incapable of predicting how things will turn out. So we parents, being of sound mind and body, have to apply the brakes. We rein in their impulsivity to protect them from themselves by setting rules and following through on those rules.

Our three teens shared four basic rules during high school: one, ask permission for weekend activities and answer questions about who, what, when, and where; two, call in to let Bill and me know their whereabouts; three, obey curfew; and four, don't drink.

Dede had no problem with any of these rules. As a tenth grader, she was organized and no stranger to a busy schedule of sports practices, after-school projects, club meetings and competitions, and the occasional doctor's appointment. If she was going to be late, she called. However, high school catapulted her into a world of dating, partying, sex, and drugs and alcohol, an intimidating path for a reserved young girl. She enjoyed dating, going to ball games and being with friends, like every other high-school teen, but opted out of those activities she knew might involve sex, drugs or alcohol, a fact her brothers and peers confirmed.

I soon realized my sweet-faced boys had fully transformed into high-school teenagers when I was driven to ask, "Who are those lanky young men with wild blond hair sleeping upstairs?" Like Dede, Andy and Mark were good students; however, they were more socially inclined than she was, meaning they liked to hang out in their boy-girl groups and party, whereas she felt uncomfortable in that type scenario. The boys agreed that most of the rules during high school were for their welfare, not for their exemplary sister's.

Getting Around the Rules

With high school now in the picture, the Y-chromosome phenomenon took on graver meaning. Andy and his antics definitely came in handy as a learning curve for me when he passed the baton to his younger brother. Once the boys were in college, they found it amusing during family gatherings to fill everyone in on how they had circumvented the rules. Their various high school sleights of hand, such as the switcheroo maneuver and the ever so popular bob-and-weave, are particularly noteworthy and some of their favorite memories.

The elder son hadn't been in high school long before he resorted to the switcheroo maneuver. This evasive tactic had been perfected early on, but I hadn't been introduced to it until my son put it in play one afternoon when he asked permission for Friday night plans.

"Hey, Mom," he said, "can I spend the night with Ben on Friday?"

"What's going on?"

"There's a game, and then we'll hang out at his house with some of the guys."

"Will his dad be home?"

"Yes."

"OK. That sounds all right to me."

Ben, meanwhile, had the same dialogue with his own dad, except he said he was spending the night with Andy. I should have called Ben's dad right after my conversation with my son, but I didn't. I checked in with him Saturday morning instead and discovered that neither boy was where they'd said they would be.

Andy had gone through the motions of asking permission and giving us details, but he gave only part of the truth. Bill and I grounded him for three days. That meant bonding with us rather than his buddies the entire next weekend.

* * *

We knew Mark was a quick study. I promised myself to be more vigilant about his whereabouts and the company he kept. Consistency in follow-through and consequences would be a top priority. Using my experience with Andy as a reference point, I thought I would be able to read my younger son like a road map. Not so. I had neglected to keep my eyes open for the unexpected.

Like his brother, Mark was a friendly fellow. However, I later realized that his cordial manner had been used, at times, to throw me off guard. He, the more talkative of the two boys, easily yielded information whereas Andy generally practiced economy of speech. Mark didn't go for the switcheroo maneuver—that I know of. He preferred the omission-for-permission method and replaced Andy's vagueness with disarming, friendly conversation.

Though he was more comfortable being straightforward than Andy, he would sometimes disguise his frankness with a chatty style. Using this ploy to maneuver me off topic, he would omit a significant detail of his plans in hopes of receiving the green light without having to mention exactly what he and his friends would be doing. Mark's derailment of my train of thought initially achieved success.

Some of his good fortune had to do with timing. Both boys knew how important that was. When they got cars of their own, this omission tactic became more effective. Even though we had a rule that everyone must give Bill and me details on activities before leaving the house, often the guys would tell me their plans as they headed out the back door.

Standing at the top of the garage steps, I would hurriedly ask them key questions. After shooting back quick replies, conveniently forgetting anything I might object to, they climbed into their respective cars. I still hear myself shouting over the roaring engines, "What did you say? You know the curfew."

The next thing I knew they were gone in a cloud of exhaust. I remained alone, frustrated as the guardian of an empty garage. I should have stopped them in their tracks, but my ingenious teenagers didn't give me time to think. Ushering them back to the den to get the necessary information would have been the right thing to do. Don't make the same mistake. Ignore their expected cries of: "I'm gonna be late." You're in charge. Your children can be inconvenienced and arrive late to their destinations.

The Teen's Weekend Plans

Although I didn't always get the information I wanted before the kids dashed out the back door, another hitch made being totally informed difficult: teenagers don't plan ahead. They hang out before deciding on the evening's entertainment, which can create a problem with curfew. We lived in Gastonia but the kids preferred Charlotte, a teen hotspot with better theaters and more movie choices. Attending the late movie there and making the twenty-mile drive home in time for a twelve o'clock curfew was impossible.

But with kids nothing is impossible. Mark asked for a later curfew every now and then. The precedent had been set by Andy before his senior year. Because it wasn't routine, I conceded to a time extension as long as Mark called to let us know when the movie began and which theater he was visiting. One more call after he left the theater sealed the deal.

To verify that he'd been where he'd said he would be, I could have asked for a ticket stub, but I trusted him. You might ask why I didn't, particularly since I'd been subject to his brother's slippery maneuvers. Maybe the high alcoholic content of the cold remedy I'd been taking for several days had clouded my senses. Or maybe I believed the look in his eyes and his usual, honest answers to my direct questions.

Roller Coaster Ride with Andy

While Andy and I came to an understanding about attending movies in Charlotte, I was still upset about our general lack of communication. Trying to extract a straight answer from my eldest son was like wading through peanut butter. At times, he would become so annoyed with my push for specifics that either we would get into a head-to-head confrontation or I would back off. More often than not, the kitchen was the scene of those incidents; therefore, unanswered questions were left floating around in the soapy water in the kitchen sink. It was time to drain the sink.

Andy's desire for freedom and his ability to handle that freedom didn't always jibe. You've already read about his junior-high in-school suspension in the United We Stand chapter. Like a typical teen, his struggle for independence continued into the upper grades. Having yet to figure out who he was and still in the process of character development, he wasn't above a creative application of the rules should the need arise.

"Mom, can I go to a party next weekend with Bob and Greg?" Andy threw his book bag on the den floor and stretched out on the sofa. Using the TV remote, he tuned into the ESPN update of the latest football scores.

"Who's having the party and where is it?" I asked as I put a casserole into the oven.

"It's at Eddie's house." Andy's eyes were glued to the TV.

"Who's Eddie and where does he live?"

"Somewhere close by. I don't know the name of the street." He retrieved his jacket from his book bag.

"Look, Andy, I don't know Eddie or where he lives." I was determined to get a straight answer.

"He's a friend. I'll find out tomorrow."

"Will his parents be home?" I cocked my head toward the den, straining to hear his reply.

"Bob says his parents are usually home at night."

"Call Eddie to find out." I moved to the doorway to make eye contact. The sludge of Jif was once again sucking around my ankles.

"I'll catch him tomorrow at school. Can I go now?" He rolled off the couch and gathered his belongings.

"OK for now but I need answers!"

Andy wasn't to be denied. His father was in the living room, ensconced in his favorite chair, reading the newspaper.

"Hey, Dad," he said, "can I go to a party with Bob and Greg?"

"Have you checked with your mother?" Bill shook his head at the stock market drop.

"Yes, sir. She said it was OK . . . she wants me to check on something," Andy mumbled the last part. "Can I go?"

"Whatever your mom says is fine with me."

The Outcome

Having yet to settle into a more mature state of mind, Andy wasn't above tinkering with the house rules. After making several inquiries, I learned that Eddie didn't have a rap sheet, so he checked out. But I failed to talk with Andy again to firm up his plans. By the time the weekend arrived, Bill and I had forgotten the party.

Andy went to Bob's house. From there the group ended up at Eddie's house. My son broke what I thought was a failsafe rule by manipulating the information to suit his objective. I hadn't given final permission, but when questioned, he pointed out that I had said OK. After hearing the answer he wanted to hear, he conveniently set aside the specifics of the broader conversation. When I probed deeper, he said he'd gotten permission from Dad, neglecting to mention to his father the context of my OK. And because I never said no, Andy grabbed the loophole. Creative application.

That, ladies and gentlemen, is the parent trap without parallel. This episode went down as the greatest case ever of parental negligence. Both parents failed to check in with one another, resulting in everyone's confusion and second-guessing over who said what when. As for the so-called loophole, it should have been summarily dismissed by the parents as ludicrous.

If this had been a court case, I would have characterized it as the Case of Parents Gone AWOL. Although Andy Banks was resourceful and creative with his answers, he clearly broke a house rule when he went to a party without permission. Not only did we follow up too late on whether Eddie's parents would be home, we forgot about the party altogether. Negligence at its worst.

Sin of all sins, Andy received no consequences. I could excuse our laxity by claiming an extremely busy schedule, problems at work, and consequently no time to follow through on the party issue. Who isn't busy or doesn't have tough days on the job? Parenting requires diligence and vigilance, pushing through the fog of a merry-go-round existence in order to remain present when dealing with your child's requests and issues. When you think about it, it's his future at stake, not yours. Bill and I failed miserably. Had we gone to trial, the verdict would have been obvious: solitary confinement with no chance of parole.

High School Curfew

When Dede reached the tenth grade, Bill and I established an eleven o'clock curfew that remained in place during the boys' high school days. With the eleventh and twelfth grades, curfews changed to eleven-thirty and midnight respectively. All three children obeyed this rule with rare exceptions. I will never forget one of those exceptions during Andy's senior year. He walked in an hour past curfew.

"Andy, where in the world have you been?" I asked. "I've been calling everywhere. Nobody knew anything. You didn't call."

"Mom, I'm sorry. The guys and I were hanging out and I lost track of time."

"Why didn't you call?" I was so angry I was shaking inside.

"When I saw how late it was, I didn't want to waste anymore time, so I came home as fast as I could. Look, I'm sorry. It won't happen again."

"You're right it won't happen again because you've lost your car for three weeks. No excuses."

"Aw, come on, Mom. That's not fair. I've never been late before. I'm sorry. I won't do it again."

"Three weeks . . . maybe a month. I don't know."

* * *

My anger was a normal reaction to fear. I imagined that he'd been in a car wreck and was lying unconscious on the side of the road. Or worse. I should have waited until the next morning when I could have calmly listened to his explanation. Although controlling my emotions was easier said than done, my ability to cope improved tenfold with some distance from the crisis. If I had dealt with Andy's late arrival the next day, I would have realized that he had never missed curfew before and that his apology had been sincere.

Since I lashed out at him, his respect for me, based on acting with fairness and reason, was shaken. I remember the deep hurt in his eyes and his exasperation. He'd been wrong but so had I. As a *mature* adult, I should have had better control. Three weeks was too long for a first violation. That punishment should be saved for a more serious offense, specifically drinking or drinking and driving. Rather than guide him, I punished Andy for the fear he had caused me; I made sure he knew who was boss.

Secondary to my not showing respect for my son was giving him a punishment that involved my participation. When I repossessed his car, I became his driver. I soon learned that his getting to school and finding a way home from after-school activities should have been his responsibility, not mine; after all, he was the offender. I could regard one week of inconvenience with a smile, but three would threaten my natural good nature.

After several days of toting Andy around to school and his other activities, I rethought my hasty decision and changed the three-week penalty to one. When I explained to him why I'd changed my mind, I also told him he would need to find someone to chauffeur him around the remainder of the week. The more I thought about the incident, the more I understood how important mutual respect between parents and children was in keeping communication lines open and relationships intact.

Underage Drinking

Another issue Bill and I revisited many times during the teenage years was drinking. My ideal world did not permit underage drinking nor did it allow my teens to attend parties without parents in attendance or where alcohol and drugs were present.

Dede attended her first and last party during her ninth grade year. When she arrived to find kids drinking and no parents in sight, she called me. She sounded so frightened that I had jumped in the van and was on my way before she'd had time to hang up. It was her first experience with kids so wasted that they were vomiting and falling into the bushes.

From early on, we had preached and preached the dangers of alcohol and drugs, making clear both our consequences and those of the law. To reinforce our message, Bill took the guys to visit the local jail when Mark was in elementary school and Andy in junior high. He wanted to show them where drinking and drugs could lead. Hugging the wall opposite the jail cells and hearing the taunts of the inmates, the boys couldn't exit fast enough.

As the older boy, Andy was the first to face high-school drinking. I couldn't say how long the jailhouse image lingered in his mind, but if he drank—of course, he did—anytime during high school, he hid it extremely well. He never denied it, nor did he confess. He did swear he didn't do drugs. My brief conversations with him when he arrived home at night never raised any red flags.

Once Bill's head hit the pillow, he was comatose. On the other hand, I was a light sleeper and usually woke up at the lightest footfall. However, some nights I didn't hear either of the boys come in. Not acceptable. I should have set an alarm clock, so I could check out their eyes for alcoholic fog and test their breaths with a goodnight kiss. Let my hindsight be your foresight.

Again and again I questioned Andy about drinking. He often gave me a humorous reply like, "Yeah, Mom, I only had a case." Further interrogation produced similar responses, so I tended to end our conversation with a warning that if I caught him, he would lose car privileges and his social life. He never admitted he drank or went to gatherings where his friends drank. My mother's intuition told me he was guilty on both counts.

When Mark became a senior, our drinking rule didn't change, but my perspective on drinking did. It didn't take long for the graduating class of 2002 to get back into their fall routine of going to football games. Afterwards, they would congregate at someone's house or hang out by the dam at a nearby lake. During that first week of school, our youngest admitted in a frank discussion with me what he and his friends did at the lake.

"Mom, you don't understand," Mark said. "Everybody drinks. I'm not gonna lie to you. I'm gonna be totally honest and tell you how it is."

"All right." I prepared myself to receive more information than I'd ever heard from any of my other children.

"You say I can't go to parties if the parents aren't home. You say I can't go anywhere there are drugs or alcohol."

"Yes, Mark. Those are the rules."

"Well, I may as well stay home and be a social dropout. I won't have any place to go. I won't have any friends. I won't have anything to do. I'm being upfront with you and this is the way it is." His voice began to rise. "I'm gonna drink. I'm telling you, so you'll know. I'm not gonna lie."

"Mark, you've been honest. I respect that, but I can't give you an answer right now. I need to talk with your dad."

"I know you and Dad are the parents; ya can't condone drinking. If you catch me, you can ground me or whatever else y'all want to do. I understand that and I'm fine with it."

I pushed the old mom to the sidelines when I didn't jump on my son with six-shooters blazing. He was telling it like it was. Maybe he was frank because I had learned to listen. Being accustomed to

Andy's runaround, I was pleasantly surprised with Mark's directness. I found it unusually refreshing even though the information itself was upsetting.

I considered Mark's dilemma and ours. I had heard the standard responses many times: Everybody does it or I'll have no social life. I didn't want to succumb to his argument and be labeled a bad parent. However, there was truth in what he said. I didn't want him to be a social outcast, yet how could I allow my child to tell me what *he* was going to do? What's more, Mark was eighteen, under the legal age limit for alcohol consumption. Frankly, I didn't know how to handle the problem.

My indecision died in committee when Bill convinced me that if Mark wanted to drink, he would find a way to do so regardless of what we did. We held a conclave and informed Mark that we could not and would not condone his drinking and furthermore that he would be held accountable if we detected one drop of alcohol on his breath.

* * *

Coupled with the drinking issue was drinking and driving. By the eleventh grade, we knew Andy drank. Common sense told us that and, too, there was that twinkle in his eye. We knew Mark drank by his own admission, even though we never smelled anything or saw any evidence. We questioned each one about drinking and driving, and each swore that he never drank and drove, that there was always a designated driver (DD).

Making that last remark was surreal. In one breath I talked about my boys' underage drinking and in the next implied they were responsible young men who demonstrated good judgment by having a sober driver. Bill and I made a difficult decision, a seemingly irrational one that suggested we'd been oxygen-deprived at birth. Underage drinking was illegal and there was no excusing it, but we did. Short of locking them in the house and having them under police surveillance, they were going to drink. That was our reality.

We believed that as long as they didn't drink and drive and as long as they knew there would be repercussions if caught, we had reached a compromise, albeit a risky one, considering the many tragic scenarios that could occur. The boys understood we were adamant about check-ins with every change of location. They knew if they were caught they would lose their cars and be stripped of all privileges. They would indeed become social outcasts, because we would send them on an all-expense-paid trip to Siberia for the remainder of their skinny lives.

Since that time in our lives, Bill and I have discovered the home breathalyzer, a device a father-friend of ours had used with his three teenage daughters to verify how much they'd drunk. He cautioned parents not to buy just any device but a reliable one. The breathalyzer worked well to severely limit, if not totally stop, his daughters' illegal drinking and drinking and driving

I wish I had known about the breathalyzer, but we didn't. If you suspect your child of drinking or drinking and driving, you have nothing to lose and everything to gain by using one. This gadget may not be the perfect answer, but it can make a difference in your child's decision to drink or how much he chooses to consume.

Music

Parenting concerns never went away. Something else always needed our attention. Andy was in high school when I became worried about the music he and Mark might be listening to and the effect it could have on them. The Banks didn't get MTV or HBO in our TV programming. Bill's reputation for being thrifty worked out well in this one instance. Still we had heard about the graphic, vulgar, and violent lyrics sung and rapped by some of the new artists.

If my guys were listening to that stuff . . . who am I kidding? However, I believed they weren't like the teens talked about in magazines or on TV talk shows who responded to song lyrics in dangerous ways by taking drugs or committing suicide. As far as my two guys were concerned, I'd seen no behavior indicating a negative influence on them. Nevertheless, this kind of unhealthy music found targets in households ranging from the lower socio-economic population to the wealthier ones. Regardless of the music's popularity, I could not and would not condone it.

Checking out the boys' music made it onto my to-do list. One day when the noise—I mean music—filled the entire upstairs and spilled into the foyer, I decided to check it out. After knocking, I entered Andy's room, pretending to look for dirty socks and underwear. The giant black speaker towers spewed enough vulgar language and graphic sexual remarks to singe my eardrums. I transformed from Laundry Mom to General Patton in the time it took Clark Kent to become Superman.

"That is the most obscene music I have ever heard!" I said.

"Mom, it's no big deal," Andy said calmly.

"Everybody listens to it," Mark chimed in from the doorway.

I wasn't going to be taken in by this standard defense. "Well, it's trash. I don't want y'all to be desensitized by that awful language and think it's OK to use it. Don't y'all know that listening to this stuff all the time can change how you think and what you do?"

"Mom, I'm just listening to it," Andy said. "It's not going to make me go crazy. Anyway, we listen to all kinds of music . . . classic rock, country."

"You're overreacting," Mark said. "We're not going to OD on drugs or something stupid like that."

"Well, I've made a new rule. If I hear that music in this house or coming from your cars, the CD is mine and its life expectancy is nil. Hand over the CD, Andy."

I confiscated the offensive CD and threw it into the garbage. I didn't care how much it cost, which was my son's primary concern. The music glorified material things, men bashing women, drugs, and murder. It spoke of death in drive-by shootings. The language was graphic, vulgar and violent, not romantic, hopeful, or upbeat like the rock music of my day . . . well, OK, there had been a few songs about motorcycle wrecks, lost love, and betrayal, but nothing like the music my guys were listening to.

Censorship and Room Checks

If you have time to listen to your children's well-stocked library of songs downloaded onto their smart phones, tablets, and whatever other electronic devices the future holds, or if you have time to research numerous musical groups whose names defy reason, you could eliminate the X-rated music in your home. Most parents don't have the time for a project of that magnitude. Even if they did, teens would find a way to tune in without their knowledge. Headphones and ear buds are only two of their options.

I couldn't trust the retail stores not to sell the guys CDs with parental advisory or explicit lyric labels, so I conducted surprise checks of their hot, trendy tunes. I trashed several more CDs, but because the job of CD censor required twenty-four-hour surveillance, many others survived. As far as I could tell, my sons remained as emotionally balanced as teens could be and physically whole except for their intermittent hearing loss, which I determined to be selective and gender-related.

Indirectly connected to the music issue is the problem of children who spend an excessive amount of time in their rooms not interacting with the family. This behavior could indicate drug- or alcohol-related problems, relationship difficulties with parents and peers, or too much time spent with the wrong people. The boys did spend time in their rooms but it was never excessive. They were either studying or listening to music. They hung out with Bill and me as much as any typical teen but spent much more time with their many friends.

Regardless, Bill and I didn't want to leave anything to chance. We checked on them periodically and never detected smoke or smelled odors beyond the norm seeping from underneath their doors. Nor did we hear demonic chants inside their poster-adorned rooms. We continued to ask questions and kept what we thought was a sufficient watch on the guys.

Without going to the extreme of bugging their rooms, thereby qualifying us as partisans of the nut patrol, we casually observed how much time they spent in their rooms. In our judgment, they were boys who exhibited no behavior beyond the boundaries of the Y-chromosome phenomenon.

More Counseling

While writing this book, I realized that I had sought counseling more often than I'd thought. On one occasion I spent eighty dollars to discover something I already knew: I was the parent; I was in charge.

Spurred on by professional validation, I understood that if I was to be in charge, I had the right to ask my children, specifically my teens,

any question—Are you taking drugs? or Are you sexually active?—
and to require an answer on the spot. The counselor added that Bill
and I needed to be available as the teen's go-to people for advice.
Whether he liked it or not, the youngster needed us to take charge,
give him our advice which, I'm sorry to say, was not always on his
agenda.

The teen years provide fertile ground for shoring up life lessons
introduced in childhood. Unaware he is suffering from an identity
crisis, the teen struggles to figure out who he is and what place he
will have in the pecking order. Because he's confused about what's
good and not good for him—he'd swear he knows everything—he's
likely to make mistakes. After all, he didn't ask to be bombarded
with the many trials of his species, such as thinking about somebody
other than himself, listening to and obeying authority, being
accountable, and handling surging hormones, to name a few. He
needs our advice and our wisdom.

As the psychologist confirmed, we must be resolute and take
charge of our children for their long term welfare. Sacrifice today,
enjoy tomorrow.

* * *

Wanting so badly to bring up good kids, I had often allowed my
insecurities, my need for approval and reassurance that I was doing
the right thing, to get in the way of doing what was best, thus
allowing my good sense to crumble. When unsure, trust your gut;
most of the time you'll be glad you did, because by taking charge
you place the odds in your favor with every issue that may arise.

Typically, my oldest son wanted an immediate response to his
requests. It didn't matter if he was in a hurry or not. However, when
he was late, his friend honking for him in the front drive, I would go

into a tailspin, grab a few details, weigh his request, and if all sounded fine, give him permission to go with his buddy.

The therapist put an end to Andy's nonsense with a second piece of advice: I didn't have to respond to a child's request right away, particularly if the request came at the last minute. He emphasized I should take all the time I needed to make a sound decision. Why I thought I had to give instant answers, I don't know

With the therapist's advice lodged in my brain, I set about parenting full steam ahead, more confident than ever. Suddenly, as if I had been jarred from a dream, I recognized that when Andy came to me wanting this or that, he would be sporting his engaging trademark: a pair of twinkling eyes and an impish grin, two telltale signs that something was afoot. With this ammo, I knew to push him for clarity of detail, take all the time I needed, no matter the urgency, to get the answers I wanted. Andy's last year of high school gave me many chances to practice what I'd learned from the therapist, plus to take advantage of one additional insight: Beware, the twinkle that charms should sound the alarm.

By Mark's senior year, I had mastered the counselor's advice. My youngest son understood that if he persisted in demanding an answer to his request, not giving me enough time to think the matter through, my answer would be an automatic no. Consequently, he came to me early with all the particulars of his plans. His adapting to this arrangement worked well for both of us, creating less stress in the household.

By then, I had come a long way. The quick-exit garage scenarios were no more. The omission-for-permission tactic had become obsolete. I called parents beforehand to see if we had the same information regarding weekend activities. If I needed to, I called them at night whether it was late or not. I remember how good it felt to achieve that kind of success, buoyed by an infusion of trust in myself and a new resolve to be in charge, to take action without distraction.

The Dust Settles

With the last cap and gown ceremony, Bill and I breathed the breath of empty nesters. We had suffered through the parental growing pains of broken rules and disrespect, of veering right when we should have gone left. Through it all, we did our best to teach our children the difference between right and wrong.

At times we'd come up short in guiding them toward safe harbors of maturity by failing to make the boys accountable. In some cases, I allowed my sensitive nature to override my common sense, doing a disservice to my children. Remember that long-term goals are best achieved by daily enforcement of the rules and consistency in accountability, which create respect for the limits parents set. You either sacrifice early or you pay later.

Bill and I managed to get it right sometimes. I recall moments of enlightened teaching when sending the kids to their rooms for breaking a rule and having them write apology notes for neighborhood pranks produced desired results. We gave them the freedom to test their options, yet reined them in by denying them car and weekend privileges. Had there been the cell phones, iPods or similar electronic gadgetry that we have today, we could have also used these items for leverage in getting them to behavior in a more desirable way.

We shared the joys of the kids' showing kindness, practicing good manners, and doing well in school. And while the do-right rule may not have taken root a hundred percent while the children lived at home, it still stands today. I keep the faith that they will eventually apply this simple philosophy to all matters in their adult lives, that their practicing it will be as natural as breathing.

Parenting is hard. I can't say that enough. And knowing how to constructively use your children's misbehavior and bad choices to teach them life lessons takes preparation. The job also requires tenacity to change what needs changing, a willingness to sacrifice, an intentional adherence to your God-given common sense that at times can be misplaced or overruled, and the stamina to weather the glares, the caustic remarks, and the inevitable storms.

And that last paragraph brings me to this simple truth: "P" is for parent, not pal. We're not in the business of being our children's friends. They have friends; they need parents. Our tough decisions cannot be diluted by being friends with them so they can stay in "like" with us. They don't know better; they don't want to know better because they can't see down the road to maturity and the good life that comes with it. We know better; therefore we parent.

Preparation is by no means a magical elixir that eliminates all the turmoil of family life. It doesn't guarantee you total success in rearing upright children. But it will fortify you with information that will help you put your best foot forward and reduce family stress. I strongly believe that striving to be good parents coupled with preparation is by far a better recipe than no preparation at all. Forearmed is forewarned.

Eighteen years seemed so far away when I'd held my firstborn. My friends had warned me that those family years would zoom by. They were right. You only have a dozen and a half years to instill the character and integrity that will steer your children toward a rewarding future as morally responsible adults. Listen to your friends. Be prepared. Tighten your boot laces and strap yourself in for the most challenging and life-altering ride you'll ever take.

* * *

Roses are true,
Daisies never tell.
Accountability is key
For your child to do well

CHAPTER SIX

FAMILY TRADITIONS
The Tie That Binds

In 1974 Bill and I spent our summer vacation with my brother Mike and his wife, and mutual friends at the coast in Cherry Grove, South Carolina. During that week my new hubby received his family nickname.

"Hey, Bill, Robin tells me you bought a Sunfish sailboat," Mike said as we turned onto Ocean Boulevard.

"Yeah, I got it a few weeks ago. Can't wait to get her in the water."

As soon as the group arrived at the single-story, oceanfront house on stilts, we changed into bathing suits and dashed to the beach. We were having a grand time cutting through the whitecaps until Bill tacked when he should have jibbed. With a jerk, the sailboat tossed all four of us into the ocean

"Look out for jellyfish!" Bill shouted as he struggled to right the boat. It was August, jellyfish season. Those nasty little critters had been thumping against the hull ever since we passed the breakers.

The sea creatures swarmed around us. The moment I felt a whisper of tentacles slide down my knee and calf, I shot out of the water like a runner off the block, scrambling onto the boat, not caring that my bikini top encircled my waist. After getting everyone on board sting-free, we set a course straight for shore, where my brother summarized the captain's inaugural voyage.

"Barnacle Bill, you sail a boat 'bout like you drive a car . . . like a bat out of hell." From that moment on, Bill became known as Barnacle Bill (the Sailor).

* * *

The beach vacation and sailboat adventure gave Bill a chance to become more comfortable with my family, since he'd lived out of town and had had little opportunity to be with everyone, except during the wedding festivities. His being christened Barnacle Bill so early after his entry into my birth family, the Gunters, was a big deal to me. As long as I can remember my older brother Mike, my younger sister Peaches, and I embraced the giving of nicknames with enthusiasm.

Some families philosophized about life's greatest truths; the Gunter clan turned to more mundane matters like the conferring of nicknames. The disparity of the two pursuits may invite a chuckle or two, but I'm smiling all the same. If the topic weren't such a vital part of who we are, I wouldn't mention it, much less devote an entire section to it.

A Tradition is Born

"Blessed Be the Tie that Binds" is a Methodist favorite. After "Jesus Loves Me," it was one of the first hymns I learned in church. There is no better way to emphasize the importance of family traditions than to say they are without question the ties that bind the family. Most of the Banks traditions centered on holidays, and included my immediate family, my parents, my siblings and their families.

However, my brother Mike played a pivotal part in starting an extended family tradition that went beyond our greater family gatherings to the bestowing of nicknames. My brother, who married and had children first, came up with nicknames for his two children, Kimberly and her younger brother Daniel, when they were teenagers. Dede, who was born one week after her cousin Daniel, was in junior high when she gave her younger brothers nicknames that have stuck to the present day.

When the entire crew got together, it was normal to hear references to Ducky (Mark), Clocky (Mark), Deech (Andy), Pea, Barney, Deeds (Dede), Bug, Rals, Skeeter, Buck, Ranger, Zippo, Poppy, Big Dede—later shortened to Bigs—and The Bruisers (Andy and Mark). Some family members were so colorful and multifaceted that more than one nickname was necessary. These names given early on in our extended family history were based entirely on affection, the creative flair of its author or a momentary whim.

Once my children and my siblings' children entered college, we took the process of giving nicknames to a new level. When a new person, a serious boy or girl friend of marriage potential, entered our ranks, one of our first demonstrations of acceptance was to confer an appropriate nickname, not an act that could be forced. Ordinarily, the task required weeks of study until someone came up with a name that revealed the essence of that person, reflecting some physical aspect of the candidate or personality trait. In some cases, if the name didn't feel right, in spite of the process, its fate was the rejection pile.

Though we were a tough group, the awarding of nicknames was done in the spirit of fun, some names more flattering than others, but all on the positive side. With the process successfully completed, the person's acceptance into the family had been confirmed with all honors duly accorded the invitee. In other words, he became an official target for jokes, jabs, and pranks.

Having a nickname provided a feeling of camaraderie within a special group. It went beyond mere acceptance to a deeper level of intimacy that said you truly matter to me. By virtue of that name, you were drawn into a private circle of trust, despite the ever present possibility of being the butt of the aforementioned modes of target practice.

You may be wondering how I got my nickname. It wasn't Mike who gave it to me but Bill, who was then twenty-seven years old. I was twenty-four. Before we married, he would visit me on his motorcycle when I lived in Chapel Hill, North Carolina. One day he overheard me call myself pea-face, so named because my face was so small. The next thing I knew he had bought me my own white, motorcycle helmet, personalized with a pea green border and the name PEA painted on the front. From then on, Bill and the rest of the Gunter clan began calling me Pea. It is with a humble heart that today I admit to more nicknames than a shark has teeth, though most were given without much forethought whatsoever. Nevertheless, I'm proud of each and every name.

Today we continue to give nicknames not only to new family members but also to many of our friends. This tradition doesn't involve travel or money. It fits any household and is easy to claim as one of your own. These special names can add a spark to your group dynamic; they're a tie that binds you closer together because you care enough to include someone in your circle of trust.

Sadly to say however, not everyone is nickname material. But if you are, the satisfaction you receive from this seemingly insignificant act comforts you so much that it stays with you wherever you go.

Fourth of July

One of our first extended family traditions began at Windy Hill, a small town located along the shoreline of South Carolina. We gathered there every year to celebrate the Fourth of July. The average attendance ranged between twelve and fourteen people, depending on births and divorces, the latter being referred to as the retirement of husbands.

The youngsters who arrived first at the beach house ran to the window searching for my younger sister Peaches. Upon her arrival, she barely had time to unbuckle her seatbelt before she was accosted by screaming, peewee pyromaniacs—that would be Daniel, Andy, and Mark—begging her to whisk them off to Bonanza Fireworks. The store was the world's largest fireworks shop under one roof, and a mother's worst nightmare. Because my sister had been childless when she'd begun this customary visit to the ammo dump, I always accompanied her. Someone had to censor any device that might blow up our portion of beach front along with any unsuspecting onlookers.

During the first years of this extravagant display of light and sound, Dede and her older cousin Kimberly, respectively pre-school and elementary ages, hid under the bed or huddled on the outside stairs, while Bill and Mike set off the monster bombs that turned everyone's eardrums to mush. However, after multiple reassurances each year that they would be safe, the little girls advanced to active participation when they timidly grasped the unlighted sparklers, and then after the moms lit them, held them stiffly at arm's length.

The guys' diverse strategies for lighting fireworks on the windy beach became a hilarious comedy act that, after Peaches's marriage, starred three adult males. Bill carefully lit the fuse only to have the wind blow it out. Mike cautioned the other two to stand back in case the fire hadn't really gone out, while the newest family member demanded his turn. We loved it. Eventually, the men perfected their routine to the point that everyone could enjoy the event without fear of permanent damage, physical or mental.

During those years of gathering to celebrate the Fourth, my children and my siblings' children were learning how to get along with one another, each child adding his particular personality to the Gunter clan's entertainment factor—we have more comedians than Facebook has friends. Over the years they eventually found their places and did so within the safe confines of a family of good sports, who loved to laugh and have fun.

Christmas Holidays: Christmas Eve

The Gathering: Lunchtime

Christmas was the core of our family traditions. The Banks bunch and extended family as it grew up were fortunate to spend Christmas together with my parents for more than thirty years. We might have been on a cruise, on an island, or in my hometown, but wherever we were, we were together. It was an arrangement not many families were lucky enough to enjoy.

After living in Durham, North Carolina, for two years, Bill and I returned to my home in Gastonia, also in North Carolina, when he took a job working for my father. When the family didn't travel to far away places, which happened more often than not, everyone packed their cars with food, gifts, and celebratory paraphernalia, and then traveled to my parents' (Bigs and Poppy's) house, which was a block away from our house. Once everyone arrived, we climbed into our cars and motored to our favorite restaurant Hayden's for lunch.

When the children became teenagers, our table conversation changed from what they ate and how we disciplined them to more adult topics that centered on the latest car wreck, speeding tickets, and girl or boyfriends. On one occasion, Mike awarded Dede a crashed Matchbox car in honor of her first fender-bender. That night he began calling her Crash, a short lived nickname due to a lack of pizzazz in creativity, which was unacceptable to the majority of the group.

After the second year of eating at the same restaurant, I decided to spice up the event by requiring everyone to wear reindeer antlers. And in keeping with the reindeer theme, I wore the blinking red nose to distinguish me as the creative director of the group. Then after several more years of sporting the less-than-attractive headwear, I found it necessary to pin small, colored balls to the antlers for a more festive look. I was born for those kinds of creative opportunities.

Bowling and Best Buy

After a lively lunch with family, we pushed back our chairs, stretched, and then headed to the local bowling alley. To ramp up the activity—as if we needed a reason to ramp—we each turned over five dollars to a pre-designated treasurer (definitely not my sons, The Bruisers), selected teams, and punched our nicknames into the computer. We were poised for battle. Our antics drew attention from the management, but our pleasant manner prevented them from taking action against us, even when we posed for a group photo on the alley wearing the reindeer headgear I required.

With the bowling championship determined, Mike, his son Daniel, and Daniel's younger cousins, Andy and Mark, made their annual visit to Best Buy for last-minute shopping. As usual, Mike allowed each boy to select one stocking stuffer. He had learned to keep a vigilant eye on the threesome after their inaugural visit years before—the boys had been in junior high and elementary school—when the devilish scamps had hidden a dozen or so CD's under the meager stack of items he'd placed in the basket.

Upon discovering their trickery, my brother responded with his best fraternity vocabulary, sending the boys into spasms of laughter. But being the good-natured fellow that he was, he paid the cashier, mentally noting to be more watchful the next Christmas. To the guy's delight, this traditional visit continued for a long time.

Years after the creation of the Best Buy tradition, Dede, then in high school; Kimberly in college; and their younger cousin Raleigh Anne (Peaches's daughter) in junior high, not to be outdone by male chauvinism, declared themselves full-fledged participants in all future Best Buy Christmas runs.

These same young women, who had once huddled together in a frightened mass during the fireworks show, had learned to stand up and be counted. Their assertiveness would go a long way toward their becoming independent individuals. Family traditions aren't just fun and games; they provide a training ground for maturity that evolves within an atmosphere of trust.

Church Service

Five o'clock church service was next on the agenda. Everyone had just enough time to get ready for the candlelight service. After a day of frivolity, we came together to worship God and be thankful for all our blessings, especially our family. Peaches, who insisted that we sit together and close to the front, went early to save two rows.

At the conclusion of the service, the congregation lighted candles row by row, and then raised them in front of their faces as they sang "Joy to the World." I always turned around to take in the mass of faces, aglow with the hope of Christmas. It was a moving service that united our entire family in spirit for a moment of perfect harmony.

Just as our families shared in the merriment of the Christmas season, we also came together during the Christmas Eve worship service. I strongly felt that this time, albeit brief, added one more knot to the cord that bound us together. Although our individual faith is personal and the places where we stand in our journeys differ, I find comfort in knowing that our Christianity represents an unbreakable tie that binds us together, no matter the trials we encounter in our lives.

Supper and THE Video

Bankses, Gunters, and my sister's family ate supper at the Banks house every year. The traditional cuisine was North Carolina pork barbecue with Black's Barbecue pink slaw, baked beans, and chips, followed by pound cake for dessert. A word of advice to any newcomer was: be sharp. The jokes and cuts flew at full throttle. Everyone was a target and adjustable armor was provided at the door each year.

As was our tradition, original poems, awards, spoofs, contests, and special requests were served up with dessert. At the conclusion of the talent show, everyone adjourned to the den to view the country Santa video, which had been professionally shot at a downtown location in Gastonia. It featured Mark, age four; Andy, age six; and

Dede, age ten. Mark was seated on Santa's right leg, Andy on his left one, and Dede standing next to Andy.

"Did you, uh, write Santi a letter?" Santa asked with a drawl and a rural accent.

"A letter?" Mark said.

"Yea. You, uh, forgot that, didn't you?" Santa then turned to Dede and Andy. "Have you written Santi a let—"

"Where's your list?" Mark asked, wanting Santa to confirm his name in the nice column of the Naughty and Nice list.

"I bet your mommy will help you write ol' Santi a letter, won't she?" At this point, Santa was ignoring Mark.

Dede and Andy nodded.

"Wh-wh-where's your list?" Mark persisted. His eyes began to blink, a tic he'd developed when agitated.

"Huh?" Santa was lost.

"Your list." Mark looked at the fur-clad man as if he'd transformed into a lump of red clay.

"Huh? Where's my list? Where's your list? That's what I'm talkin' 'bout." Santa cocked his head in utter confusion.

"I don't have no lis-tes." Mark began to sway.

"Ya don't?" The once jolly old elf was losing it.

Mark twisted around to look Santa dead in the eyes. "Where's your list?"

"Huh? Jus' whatever you, uh, want to name it, uh."

Mark eased forward again and sat stock still except for the twitching of his blue-gray eyes. He stared straight ahead into the camera, brow knitted and deep in thought. The only sound in the room was the buzz coming from the studio speakers.

Suddenly Santa asked, "Candy canes, anybody?"

The spell was broken. The boys slid off Santa's lap to receive their sugar fix, all three children thanking him as they walked away.

No matter how often we played the tape, we fell apart in renewed hysterics each time we heard Mark's bad grammar, "I don't have no lis-tes," and watched his dazed expression. Old Santi had clearly failed Santa school because he couldn't figure out that Mark was referring to his behavior list and not his toy list. The video has become famous throughout town and friends have requested special viewings. It is without question a family treasure and remains under heavy guard in the Banks video vault.

Traditions such as bowling, the Best Buy run, and watching a beloved video are simple ones, yet they bring a large family together with little expense and a whole lot of camaraderie.

Christmas Day: Morning Ritual, Lunch, and Diversions

Christmas morn arrived later as the children grew older. The youngest cousins stifled their excitement as the older ones snoozed away all the fun and games that had lasted well into the night. After each household opened gifts, we hopped in our cars, clad in nightgowns, boxers, and t-shirts, to visit one another and check out the loot.

We then cleaned up our respective houses. The process was interrupted by preparations for Christmas lunch, which would be served at 1:00 P.M. sharp, per house orders. We circled the dining room table holding hands as my mother blessed the food and the family. With the group amen, Andy and Mark quickly broke ranks to be first at the buffet before Uncle Mike. This happened without fail every year. My brother had been known to scrape the entire marshmallow topping off the sweet potato casserole, which left my boys plotting revenge.

Amidst the din of family chatter and settling in at the table, we opened Peaches's customary Chinese poppers filled with paper crowns, fortunes, and trinkets. We were quite the regal group in the formal dining room, using Christmas china and crystal, while wearing colorful, pointy hats. We loved our traditional activities which took place like a choreographed dance.

An Unexpected Family Event

Before we knew it, my children, Mike's and Peaches's children had entered high school and college. These years introduced a new tradition based upon an unexpected event that either took place spontaneously during the holiday or happened during the previous year. If the event occurred during the previous year, some clever soul, and there were many, would seize the opportunity during our Christmas celebration to creatively make fun of whoever was central to that event. These one-time occurrences would later be retold at family gatherings and thereby become part of the family lore.

I will never forget the time during the Christmas holidays when Peaches offered eighteen-year-old Mark a deal he couldn't refuse: cut his blond Afro for a hundred bucks. Accustomed to being in control, Peaches could not abide Mark's hair-do, telling him that he and Bozo the Clown shared a family resemblance. When Poppy, Mark's grandfather, matched her hundred, the deal was struck.

After dinner, we transformed the foyer into a mini barber shop. Mark, perched on a stepstool, was eager to sacrifice his golden locks in exchange for lining his pockets with a more desirable kind of gold.

I got the craft scissors—the only ones I could find—from the kiddy drawer, gave them to Peaches, and then went to find Bill's hair clippers, which I passed over to my sister- in-law. Everyone gathered around. Mark was enjoying the buzz of activity until he felt the clippers zoom up the side of his head.

"I agreed to a haircut, not a Mohawk," he cried. A three-inch bald spot appeared behind his right ear.

Advice bounced from one spectator to the next. Though there was no plan—Peaches was busy cutting wherever the spirit moved her and my sister-in-law was obviously on a tear—my son was much improved, not to mention two hundred dollars richer. Weezie, an eighty-year-old member of our guest family, had so much fun she accepted the invitation to permanently join our Christmas celebration. Where else could you have found live entertainment of such high quality on Christmas Eve?

Anticipation is a large part of any pleasure. We never knew what unexpected event might take place during the holidays. Patience and control (no spilling the beans) are prerequisites for any surprise, especially for those scheduled for months down the road. A healthy sense of humor on the part of the instigator keeps the surprise in good taste. Who doesn't love the creativity that goes into a harmless joke, clever prank or amusing activity? Well, maybe the recipient is not as gung-ho about being the brunt of the humor as the others are about viewing it, but these moments help us learn to laugh at ourselves, and trust in our friends and the love of family. It's healthy to slow down, take a less serious look at life, and laugh a lot while doing it.

One More Extended Family Tradition

Although Christmas was a much-anticipated holiday for our crew, our sports-minded families enjoyed other traditions, such as attending the ACC (Atlantic Coast Conference) basketball tournament. This event was not a legitimate holiday, but we deemed it so when we allowed our kids to skip school to cheer on their favorite teams. When family members lived far from each other, holding frequent reunions was difficult. The trek to Greensboro or Charlotte, North Carolina for the games strengthened the family bond.

Because of busy lives, marriages, and babies, we no longer attend the tournament for reunion purposes. But during that era, the ACC tournament gave my family an opportunity to be involved in other family members' lives, to celebrate their successes and sympathize with them over disappointments. Face-to-face attention and friendly hugs added yet another knot in the tie that bound us together.

* * *

The subject of stress comes to mind when talking about family holidays and family togetherness. It is very rare when every member of the extended family comes together for holidays. When children are small, some parents prefer to develop their own traditions. At Christmastime, for example, they often stay home to have Santa, and then later travel to grandmother's house. In many cases, when the family dynamics become more complex, such as the addition of in-laws, choices have to be made where to go when. It's oftentimes a trade-off. Holidays themselves are stressful times in our lives, so it's best to be flexible and go with any unexpected turn of events.

Families by their very natures have diverse personalities with differing opinions and annoying habits, all of which can sabotage a family gathering in a nanosecond. There may be an Aunt Maude who thinks she knows everything or an Uncle Toby who smells or a cousin Susie who whines all the time or sits around all day. The bottom line is they're family and you love them regardless of their imperfections. So when you pack your suitcase to travel, don't forget to bring your positive attitude, one that respects fellow members of the group and treats them as friends. This formula for healthy behavior is vital to the survival of family traditions and the family as well.

You could expose me right away as the great pretender if I have implied that the Gunter group get-togethers were uniquely stress-free, all fun no tension. Our group was just as dysfunctional as the next, but who wants to hear all that stressful stuff? Our moments of discord usually fizzled away in a short time. Today I don't take family for granted because I know that not everyone has a family to share the good and bad times with.

Exclusively the Banks Family

A favorite Banks family tradition was spending the Easter holidays at Myrtle Beach, South Carolina. We sunned on the beach, shopped at golf and clothing stores, and relaxed on the couch while watching whatever golf tournament or other sports event happened to be on TV. Every year we attended early service at the First United Methodist Church. A full choir accompanied by a twenty-piece orchestra created a worship service of pure, listening pleasure. Afterwards, we headed to a local restaurant for a much anticipated pancake breakfast with all the cholesterol boosting side orders we normally avoided.

Taking a break from the extended family is a good thing. Everyone can use a little space to refuel, recharge, and recover. I always looked forward to a change of scenery with fewer personalities to manage and a noise level a decibel or two lower. Our traditional family activities then as now still give us pleasure and provide entertainment that we claim as solely Banks time.

Thinking about these traditional gatherings and the time spent with immediate and extended family, I better understand how they influenced who we have become and how we relate to each other. The outings provided the security of belonging to something unique and personal. To this day, being in a family rooted in tradition fills me with a profound sense of well-being.

Diversity

My family of five with one mom and one dad isn't necessarily the stereotypical family these days. Single-parent families, families with disabled members, families with grandparents as caretakers, or families with two moms or two dads create a variety of possibilities when talking about creating traditions. Just as there are many different kinds of families, there are as many diverse ways to create meaningful traditions for each of those families.

Traditions can be on a grand scale like vacationing in exotic places. They can also be as simple as a weekly walk in the neighborhood with an uncle, monthly talks on the phone with a relative that lives out of town, watching a favorite TV show with crazy Aunt Gladys when she comes for her summer visit, an anticipated chat with grandpa about the olden days when he just happens to show up at suppertime, baking cookies with children every Saturday morning, or playing board games with Grammy.

A family with a disabled or handicapped member might not be able to take part in traditions that require a great deal of physical activity or mental ability, but the family members can enjoy traditional fellowship at a handicap accessible park or other special-needs facilities.

Now that I'm a grandmother—joy of all joys—I love visiting the duck pond or going to the movies, the park or the museum when my daughter brings the "adorables" to town. Traditional activities like these, though simple in nature, provide cherished memories for everyone.

Actually, any customary activity in which family members come together, no matter the kind of family, creates a tie that binds them as one with an invisible force that soothes and delights with anticipation and expectation.

The Banks Bunch

The Banks and extended family rituals gave our children a sense of belonging. That feeling was reinforced by the anticipation of expected and unexpected activities, for example the priceless Banks Christmas video or joking with clan members or plotting capers yet to be imagined. Our traditions go to the core of the family circle to provide a sense of well-being that wraps us in a hug so tight that burdens fall away, if only briefly, and contentment nestles into our bones. What a gift, one to be maintained and protected at all costs.

At this point in my life, the passage of time seems to be stuck in fast-forward. So much is happening so quickly. Our entire family dynamic seems to have changed overnight. Even though it's not true, I feel that a month doesn't go by without someone in the group either getting married, having a baby, moving to a new house, or starting a different job. The once familiar traditions that have faded away will be replaced by new ones. Families, just like countries, find pride and a sense of identity in their diverse traditions. Individual members become the roots that support the family tree. Common memories connect us for a lifetime.

* * *

Roses by the dozen,
'Tis a delight to behold.
Family traditions,
'Tis food for the soul.

EPILOGUE

Discovery: Parenting is a process whereby you exchange the physical demands of young children for the emotional challenges of older ones. Each phase is no easier or more important than the one before it, merely different as your child moves towards independence. New goals are added as your family grows. Your good preparation and common sense, your commitment to hard work and sacrifice, and your love and nurture are the constants needed to meet every goal.

More than likely, once you're in the throes of the never-ending demands of caring for your newborn, balancing your time between child and husband—your child pulling, your husband pushing—you'll hear yourself cry out: "I can't do this twenty-four seven for eighteen years." It's normal. This happens to all of us at one time or another.

But wouldn't it be great if a parenting genie set up shop in your house to take care of all the difficult times from the moment you bring that adorable package home? Yes, it would, but where's the challenge in that? Though I can't put a genie at your fingertips, I can make you an offer you can't refuse: adopt the wisdom of preparation before that erratically swimming sperm collides with the patiently awaiting egg. Take heart that you can do this imposing task called child rearing and that you will be more successful than you think. Remember: Knowledge is bliss; ignorance is for the birds. You can quote me on that.

Knowledge is also power; it is that critical edge of *knowing* that gives you time to adjust your attitude in order to soften the bumps in the road that creates a smoother ride, a discovery I'm convinced all you future and current parents would die for if you knew the journey that awaits you. This book has given you a glimpse of that journey. Once *Get a Grip II* is available, you'll read about five additional parenting tips: danger zones, safety and rescue nets, recharging your battery, good manners and habits, and seeds of faith.

Obviously, I didn't stumble across any parenting genie, not even a mere parenting princess. Nor could I find the how-to manual that surely the nurse gave me right before my departure from the hospital. So I dove into the parenting waters weighed down by heavy baggage. With great effort, I was able to surface and shed some of that baggage. I killed Attila the Hun—R.I.P—and embraced a more thoughtful Mona Lisa. Nevertheless, even today, I frequently have to mentally shift gears every time a volatile subject is introduced, so I don't fall back on old habits of behavior.

Never did I give up on parenting. Neither should you. That's not to say the thought didn't pass through my mind a time or two. Despite Bill's and my not reaching the degree of success I desired with a united front, we have committed ourselves to achieving this goal before the children put our ashes in matching urns on some lucky offspring's mantel.

You now understand the necessity of securing a united front, being patient, admitting what's not working and then making changes, and above all following through on your decisions. And if all these pieces of the puzzle aren't fitting together just so one particular day—your nervous system gauge registers an emotional overload—I recommend eating lunch with the girls. Your buddies will help you reset those tattered emotions, so you can jump back on that merry-go-round, recharged and ready to brave the home front with a full stomach and a clearer head. What would we women do without our girlfriends? Don't answer that question; there's already enough sadness in the world.

Those eighteen years with kids at home will be like a snap in time. Before you know it, they will be gone; the walls of your house will echo far fewer footfalls and quieter conversations. Slow down and cherish them. Embrace living in the present, savoring the good and handling the mistakes and unpleasant confrontations with confidence. Don't allow the daily grind to get you down. As long as you stay headed in the right direction, though you fall off the path, tomorrow offers another day for renewed resolve, another day to get it right or do it better. Hang in there, because rewards eventually come.

I wanted *Get a Grip* to be an informal guide to prepare future parents. When I finished the book, I realized it was also a source of comfort for on-the-job parenting blues. Whenever you need a dose of reassurance, you can take the book off the shelf, turn to any chapter, and wrap yourself in it the way my daughter sought comfort in her satin-trimmed baba. It will remind you that you're human, and that regardless of your mistakes, you're still a good parent, who shouldn't fear scarring your child forever or seeing his picture on the post office wall.

Looking back at how we parented, I can say that Bill and I did OK. We had our successes, especially in passing down to our children integrity, trustworthiness, and a respect for fellow human beings. We also made mistakes, some more costly than others, though none fatal. Preparation could have lessened if not totally prevented some of those mistakes. Take comfort in that.

To be sure, we left our children to deal with the residual effects of our parental missteps: misunderstandings, less-than-sterling decisions, and unsound behavior. Time and patience will unveil our children's futures as they enter the world of jobs, marriage, and children of their own. It will be up to them to add the finishing touches to their final transformations as they meet the changes life will require.

Change can be good. The maturation process continues for all of us. We should never stop learning and improving who we are. But one thing will never change: I will continue to parent, even though today parental involvement in our children's lives looks more like advice-upon-request than the former, unsolicited advice-upon-demand. Bill and I remain united on this. And unless and until the children are transported to another star system, I will be planted firmly on this Earth should they need to call me or click on my name.

Finally, discard the pursuit of perfection if this is your mode of operation; rather, allow common sense to be your guide. Your children's lives will be shaped by words of encouragement and bouts of anger, times of praise and those of disappointment, uplifting laughter and heartbreaking tears, moments of joy and periods of sadness. In view of that reality, I offer you these truths:

You prepare.
You do the best you can.
You strive to be a reflection of all
You want your child to be.
You live with your eyes on God.
You love unconditionally.